Online Language Teaching: Crises and Creativities

The book series "Developing Online Language Pedagogies" covers online teaching and learning in a way that makes it relevant to practitioners and researchers. The first volume, "Online Language Teaching: Crises and Creativities," exemplifies this approach by collecting creative and altruistic responses of language educators and organisations to the challenges of the Covid-19 pandemic. Colleagues from Austria, Canada, the Czech Republic, Germany, Korea, Spain, the UK and the USA present their individual and institutional reactions to the need for rapid staff training in times of lockdown and an emergency move to online language teaching. The volume culminates in a collaborative conclusion where all the authors jointly reflect on exceptional circumstances and how the crisis can give rise to creative solutions.

Dr Ursula Stickler is a Senior Lecturer in German in the School of Languages and Applied Linguistics at the Open University (UK). Her research centres around online and independent language learning, teacher training and the use of new and qualitative methods in online learning research. She is expert consultant with the European Centre for Modern Languages (ECML).

Dr Martina Emke coordinates the academic staff development programme for Netzwerk hdw nrw, an association of twenty universities of applied sciences in North Rhine-Westphalia, Germany. Previously, she worked as a language teacher in further education, higher education and in a vocational school. Her research interests include posthuman digital education, networked learning, and the use of social media in language teaching and learning.

Developing Online Language Pedagogies Series

Series Editors: Ursula Stickler & Martina Emke

Ursula Stickler & Martina Emke: *Online Language Teaching: Crises and Creativities*

Adrian Leis & Matthew Wilson: *Screen Media in Foreign Language Education*

More information about titles in this series can be found at
https://www.castledown.com/academic-books/book-series/developing-online-language-pedagogies

Online Language Teaching

Crises and Creativities

Edited by

Ursula Stickler
The Open University

Martina Emke
The Open University

Melbourne – London – Tokyo – New York

4th Floor, Silverstream House, 45 Fitzroy Street Fitzrovia, London W1T 6EB, United Kingdom
Ground Level, 470 St Kilda Road, Melbourne, Victoria 3004, Australia
2nd Floor Daiya Building, 2-2-15 Hamamatsu-cho, Minato-ku, Tokyo 105-0013, Japan
447 Broadway, 2nd Floor #393, New York NY, 10013, United States

First published 2023 by Castledown Publishers, London

Information on this title:
www.castledown.com/reference/9781914291173

DOI: 10.29140/9781914291173

Online Language Teaching: Crises and Creativities
© Ursula Stickler & Martina Emke (Editors), 2023

All rights reserved. This publication is copyright. Subject to statutory exception and to the provisions of relevant collective licencing agreements, no reproduction, transmission, or storage of any part of this publication by any means, electronic, mechanical, photocopying, recording or otherwise may take place without prior written permission from the author.

Typeset by Castledown Design, Melbourne
ISBN: 978-1-914291-17-3 (Paperback)
ISBN: 978-1-914291-16-6 (Digital)

Castledown Publishers takes no responsibility for the accuracy of URLs for external or third-party internet websites referred to in this publication. No responsibility is taken for the accuracy or appropriateness of information found in any of these websites.

Contents

List of contributors   vii

Preface   x

Chapter 1   1
Introduction
Ursula Stickler and Martina Emke

Chapter 2   8
Teacher training in times of Covid-19
Pauline Ernest & Sarah Heiser

Chapter 3   28
Creating presence in remote learning: Moving a participatory f2f workshop concept online
Aline Germain-Rutherford, Banafsheh Karamifar, & Tomáš Klinka

Chapter 4   45
Webinars as a rapid response for training language teachers to teach online in 2020
Jackie Robbins & Joseph Hopkins

Chapter 5   64
"Moving your language teaching online" Toolkit: Teachers' early reflections on their experience and skills
Karina von Lindeiner-Stráský, Hélène Pulker, & Elodie Vialleton

Chapter 6   82
Transitioning to online teaching: Language teacher wellbeing during the Covid-19 crisis
Sun Shin

Chapter 7   98
Microblending as a response to Covid-19
David Bish

Chapter 8 113
Collaborative conclusion
Ursula Stickler and Martina Emke and all authors

Index *129*

List of contributors

Dr David Bish began teaching English online over 20 years ago and has since worked as a teacher trainer, Director of Studies and Materials designer. David's work was twice shortlisted for the British Council ELTONs awards. A passionate conference speaker, David stays close to the classroom face to face and online, trailing his materials and teaching online daily through lockdown.

Dr Martina Emke coordinates the academic staff development programme for Netzwerk hdw nrw, an association of twenty universities of applied sciences in North Rhine-Westphalia, Germany. Previously, she worked as a language teacher in further education, higher education and in a vocational school. For the European Centre for Modern Languages (ECML) Martina has worked as a teacher educator, project co-coordinator and materials developer. Her research interests include posthuman digital education, networked learning, and the use of social media in language teaching and learning.

Pauline Ernest was Director of the Language Program at the Centre for Modern Languages at the Universitat Oberta de Catalunya and is co-coordinator of the ICT-REV Training and consultancy offer at the European Centre for Modern Languages (ECML). Her research interests include language learning in online environments, computer supported collaborative work, and teacher training in ICT use in the language classroom.

Aline Germain-Rutherford, PhD, is Professor in the Faculty of Education at the University of Ottawa. She is also Adjunct Professor in the Faculty of Education at Charles University, Prague. Her research addresses faculty development, second language pedagogy, speech technology and the integration of active pedagogy into online learning practices. She is the recipient of the Canadian 3M National Teaching Fellow Award for excellence and leadership in higher education.

Sarah Heiser is a Senior Lecturer in the School of Languages and Applied Linguistics at the Open University UK. She is Associate Dean, Student Tuition of her Faculty and a Senior Fellow of the Higher Education Academy (SFHEA). She is an experienced academic line manager with interests in technology enhanced language learning and teacher development by experiential learning in online spaces.

Joseph Hopkins is the Director of the Centre for Modern Languages at the Universitat Oberta de Catalunya. He is also one of the coordinators of the ICT-REV Training & Consultancy offer of the European Centre for Modern Languages (ECML). His main areas of expertise are web-based language teaching and learning, language teaching management, and language teacher development.

Banafsheh Karamifar, PhD, is researcher and part-time professor in both the Faculty of Arts and the Faculty of Education of the University of Ottawa, Canada. Her research interests include technology-enhanced language learning, literacy in higher education, discourse analysis, and corpus linguistics.

Tomáš Klinka: PhD in Sciences of Education, Head of the Department of French language and literature, Faculty of Education, Charles University, Prague, Czech Republic. Main interests and research topics: assessment, error analysis and ICT in French as a foreign language learning/teaching. Active language teacher (FLE) of 11-15 years old pupils in a public school in Prague.

Dr Karina von Lindeiner-Stráský's teaching and research specialises in aspects of Modern German Literature and Linguistics. She is Senior Lecturer and Head of German at the School of Languages and Applied Linguistics at the Open University and has published widely on political literature and memorialisation. Her current research focuses on communication in the digital world.

Marta González-Lloret is a Professor of Applied Linguistics at the University of Hawai'i. Her main areas of research are at the intersections of technology, Task-based Language Teaching and L2 pragmatics. She is co-editor of the John Benjamins *Task-based Language Teaching* book series and editor of the NFLRC book series *Pragmatics & Language Learning*.

Dr Hélène Pulker is a Senior Lecturer in French in the School of Languages and Applied Linguistics at the Open University (UK) with 16 years of experience in designing and writing materials for distance and online language learning and teaching. Her main research focuses on the use and adaptation of Open Educational Resources for language teachers' professional development.

Jackie Robbins, PhD, is a Lecturer at the Universitat Oberta de Catalunya where she coordinates several English-as-a-foreign-language courses. She is a member of the European Centre for Modern Languages ICT-REV project team which supports language teaching and learning in Europe. Her research interests include online language learning, learner engagement and special needs language learners in online contexts.

Sun Shin is currently working as a Pre-doc research assistant at the University of Graz on the FWF- funded project "The Psychological Capital of Foreign Language Teachers." Alongside this project, she is pursuing her PhD aimed at exploring teacher wellbeing in South Korea. She is a certified CELTA teacher and taught English as a foreign language in South Korea and Thailand.

Dr Ursula Stickler is a Senior Lecturer in German in the School of Languages and Applied Linguistics at the Open University (UK). Her research centres around online and independent language learning, teacher training and the use of new and qualitative methods in online learning research. She is expert consultant with the European Centre for Modern Languages (ECML).

Dr Elodie Vialleton is a Senior Lecturer in French in the School of Languages and Applied Linguistics at the Open University. Her main research areas are the use of naturally occurring speech in language teaching, and online and distance language teaching: online learning designs, distance pedagogy, curriculum development and materials design, and distance language teacher development.

Preface

Marta González-Lloret

This volume is a collection of research and experiences in a variety of settings (Czech Republic, Canada, UK, Spain, Korea) to illustrate how language teachers globally responded to the requirements of moving language teaching online. The chapters are highly relatable to many educators that find themselves in the tension that the authors describe between 1) being a researcher and collecting precious data in unprecedent times of online language education (to contribute to world knowledge and a better-informed future); and 2) being a collaborative educator and supportive colleague that needed to help resolve immediate, very real, needs.

This volume is not only a recount of valuable personal experiences, but it also offers an overview of studies published by researchers, questionnaires issued by educational institutions, and help-sites offered publicly, to paint a view of how the world reacted to the move into online education (see Chapter 2 by Ernest and Heiser). In addition, this volume offers valuable resources and tools that were created for emergency remote teaching (ERT): an attempt to provide temporary access to instruction and instructional support in a manner that is quick to set up and is readily available during an emergency (Hodges et al., 2020) and are still available and current. These resources are highly relevant and useful for any language teacher still teaching languages online or who wants to include some technology in a face-to-face curriculum. These resources exemplify the dichotomy presented by the volume editors between crisis and creativity and present their visions for the future after the pandemic. For examples, see the UK Open University's "Moving your language teaching online" (Chapter 5) and the ICT-REV Inventory of tools and open educational resources (https://www.ecml.at/ict) by the European Centre for Modern Languages (Chapter 4).

This volume offers suggestions that are not just descriptive of what was done, but that can serve for any future moves from face-to-face to online learning. This is extremely useful for the hundreds of language teachers all over the world that now either want, or are "gently pushed" by their administration, to continue online language teaching.

Since the editors and authors are teacher educators, the main topic of teacher training is featured prominently throughout the entire volume.

The volume demonstrates that the move to online language teaching offered both opportunities and challenges that required a high level of resilience from teachers and students (Salmon, 2014). Robbins and Hopkins (Chapter 4) illustrate how some of the consequences of having to move teacher training online had a positive impact such as the evolution of a small-scale program to a video-streaming project that could reach thousands of teachers in need of online teaching training.

In line with previous publications (e.g., Gonzalez-Lloret, Canals, & Pineda, 2021), this volume shows that language teachers are resilient and flexible. During difficult times, teachers are able to adapt and prevail. In their special issue, González-Lloret et al. (2021) showed how the pandemic had affected teachers from all over the world (from Poland to Malaysia to Colombia, Mexico, Spain, Czech Republic, and the USA) regardless of type of institution or type of student (universities, pre-schools, immersion programs, and language centers for students with autistic disorder and Down Syndrome), and how collectively language educators were trying to make sense of new practices. The volume illustrated the teachers' journey and that of their students through innovation and change and showed how some of the tools and ideas implemented during the first months of the pandemic could be adopted in traditional face-to-face classrooms. This volume goes further by examining closer the impact that teacher training (or a lack of) had on the ERT of languages and proposing changes to apply to future teacher education. Modifications that have already resulted in improved and enhanced new approaches to the design of professional development (see Chapters 3, 4, and 5).

During the first months of the pandemic, in a move to help teachers become ready for online teaching, an overwhelming amount of learning resources (e.g., tips about teaching online, different tools and how to use them) were available to teachers from institutions (their own and others, See MIT's Teach remote website), academic journals (e.g., Foreign Language Annals), academic organizations (AATSP, TESOL), and from textbook editorials. Although much needed, these became overwhelming, and teachers did not know how to choose which ones to give the little extra time that they had, many times at the expense of personal and family time. This was without a doubt a stressful time, as discussed by Shin in Chapter 6.

Shin's chapter brings to light the utmost importance of teachers' mental state and wellbeing during times of disruption of normal teaching practices. As the author explains, teacher wellbeing is closely linked to teaching quality and positive student experiences. When teachers are stressed, their relationships with students suffer, which in turn affects students' behaviors and performance. Shin reports on the coping strategies of four teachers in Korea at different points during the pandemic. As she states, although problem-focused, adaptive coping (e.g., seeking social support) improves a situation, emotion-focused maladaptive coping strategies (e.g., ignoring the stressor) provide temporary breathing space but negatively affect wellbeing in the long run. The stressors reported by Shin were those described all over the world during the first months of lockdowns: lack of clear communication by the administration (e.g., the uncertainty of how long the situation was going to last), loss of control in classes (e.g., students' refusing to turn on cameras and/or microphones), and issues with technology (e.g., overload servers, technology not working as expected). As difficult as the ERT was, it seemed to get better/easier with time. Similarly, institutional surveys presented by Germain-Rutherford, Karamifar, and Klinka in Chapter 3, conducted longitudinally in 2020 and 2021, show an evolution through the months of the pandemic towards more positive attitudes concerning online teaching, and an added ability to cope and adapt to the new situation.

However, in May 2021, the results of a survey presented by Ernest and Heiser (Chapter 2) of over 5000 teaching professionals conducted by the EU School Education Gateway Online and distance learning still showed that teachers needed support mainly with more free resources and tools from educational technology companies, clear guidance from administration, and quick lessons on online teaching. These results align with teachers' concerns identified by von Lindeiner-Strásky, Pulker, and Vialleton (Chapter 5) addressing the constraints and possibilities of the online medium (e.g., the number of tools to use, class organization, issues with assessment, learners' motivation to fully participate and turn on their cameras and mics). Both results strongly support the importance of preservice education and sustained professional development, which needs to include a technological component. This type of training is needed not just so that teachers know how to use tools and techniques that may facilitate their planning time and their everyday teaching, but so that they can make critical decisions about what is most beneficial for their particular students, in their particular context, and what is feasible given learners' and institutions' access to technology, internet access, and support. In an ideal world, all governments would make a commitment to online education, one that is backed by allocating funding for curricular changes, digitalization, and faculty development programs for sustainable and high-quality online education. For a glimpse of hope, see the case of the Czech Republic's efforts to address the post-pandemic new realities of education and their job market (Chapter 3).

When discussing wellbeing, we need to consider not just teachers' wellbeing but also learners' wellbeing. During the first months of online classes, students felt isolated and depressed in great part because their syllabi for ERT were not designed to be effective online courses. As Germain-Rutherford, Karamifar, and Klinka explain in Chapter 3, the concept of 'distance' can be reflected in not only the geographical distance, but in the structure of the curriculum, the level of dialogue between teachers and students, and the degree of autonomy that is expected from students. Although teachers tried to minimize the distance by engaging in dialogue with students, most of the time their syllabi were not structured to facilitate dialogue between students, and students were not ready to take control of much of their learning and be autonomous, because we had deprived them of most of their autonomies in traditional face to face classrooms. We tell learners what to learn, what to do inside and outside of classroom, and how they have to produce it for assessment. As a consequence, learners have barely any autonomy or control over their learning.

When well designed, online learning may actually help bring students together in a way that only technology can. For some of our students, staying connected (to their friends) means texting on the phone, sharing moments of their life through pictures and videos, revealing the important as well as the mundane parts of their lives. However, most educators did not take advantage of the technology that students were already using to make their courses more engaging spaces. For an online course to be successful, it is essential that students feel a sense of presence. As Germain-Rutherford, Karamifar, and Klinka state in Chapter 3, (quoting Garrison & Anderson, 2003) presence can be defined as "the ability of participants in a research community to project themselves socially and emotionally, in all dimensions of their personality, through the medium they use" (Garrison & Anderson, 2003, p.55). For this, a socio-cognitive presence (transactions between students to accomplish class activities), a socio-affective presence developed by the participants, and a pedagogical presence produced by moderation and facilitation of course content by the teacher need to be fostered.

Another idea that emerges through the chapters is teachers' concern for language assessment and student evaluation. We can see an evolution of how assessment was perceived and integrated during the ERT and afterwards. At the beginning of the ERT, exams (including final exams) were waived in many institutions. Many teachers tried to transfer their paper and pencil exams to online platforms and soon realized that this was not a productive way to assess learners. Teachers complained that students looked at the book, copied answers, worked with other students, etc., therefore, assessment became the largest challenge for some teachers and institutions. Although a difficult-to-solve issue for some teachers and institutions that focused on finding software that could minimize "cheating", for others, it became an opportunity to do away with traditional, formal exams and implement continuous assessment in more creative and authentic ways (e.g., self-assessment, performance-based assessment, projects, portfolios, audio and video recordings). Personally, I hope that some of these more student-centered, language performance assessment practices are permanently integrated into language curricula.

Regardless of the circumstances, teachers are always looking for tools and techniques that can be applied right away and that reduce our planning time, facilitate teaching, and help us keep learners motivated. However, no matter how useful the technology is, it should never be the driving force of a language curriculum. A language curriculum should be based on sound methodological and pedagogical choices. Activities and materials should maximize the potential for learning based on principles of second language acquisition (e.g., the need for rich input, the possibilities for output, provision of timely feedback, and oral and written interaction) and well-thought frameworks for online teaching (e.g., Stickler & Hampel, 2015). The technology should complement, enhance, and make those choices possible. Both the technology and the activities should be, first and foremost, effective for language learning. That said, there are other elements that can help a language online course be successful, many of them are highlighted in the chapters in this volume.

Some of the key elements for teacher success in online language teaching are:

- Institutional support for online teaching (e.g., economic investment, tech support, resources).
- Teacher education and technology training that is short, impactful, and fosters collaboration (Gacs, Goertel, & Spasova, 2020).
- Community support (e.g., other teachers locally and remotely, trainers, parents).
- Sustained social interaction (e.g., sharing outside the curriculum).
- Tools, strategies, and techniques to alleviate the larger workload of online courses.
- Teaching approaches that allow for collaborative, interactive, and student-centered learning.
- Accepting the role of facilitator rather than knowledge provider.
- Open mindedness and willingness to explore and test new techniques, tools, and activities (see Chapter 7 for suggestions of activities).
- Freedom to apply technologies as best suit their style of teaching and knowledge frameworks.
- Promoting teacher's wellbeing (e.g., administrative support for teaching, feeling of control, support from peers) (See Mercer & Gregersen, 2020, for more on this topic).
- Providing teachers with coping mechanisms such as positive reappraisal so that they can reframe a challenging situation as an opportunity or feel grateful by downward social comparison (i.e., seeing how other people, institutions, or countries are in worse situations) (see Chapter 6 by Shin).

In addition, teachers should also consider some key elements for student success in online language learning such as:

- Access to technology and a fast and stable Internet connection.
- Well planned lessons (methodological choices first, then technology to realize those).
- Lots of open communication between teacher-students(-parents).
- Appropriate multimodal input (at the right level, critically chosen from the overabundance that exists in Internet).
- Opportunities for oral and written production, including interaction and collaboration (see González-Lloret, 2020, for examples).
- Provision of effective and timely feedback (both for oral and written production). Several tools are proposed in this volume.
- Space for social interaction (e.g., showing your pets, favorite item in your room), also valuable for spontaneous language output.
- Emotional support (e.g., spaces for commiseration, peer-empathy) (see Mercer, 2021, for more on this topic).

This volume closes with a final chapter that is highly creative. To my knowledge, this is the first instance of a volume in which all authors collaboratively wrote the final summary chapter. The volume editors extracted common trends and topics from all chapters and created a series of questions that all authors answered in a synchronous collaborative Google document. As the volume editors state "We believe that thinking together creates more valuable, more accessible and longer lasting insights" (p. 4). The result is a rich closing chapter in the authors' voices that gives the reader an unusual look into the author's own experiences during the pandemic, their inspiration, and their expectations for the chapters. The authors also reflect on the links to and commonalities with other chapters and on the opportunity to write the final chapter together. Lastly, and I believe one of the most important conclusions of this volume, the final chapter emphasizes that theory, evidence-based research, and spaces for teacher training are at the heart of effective online language teaching, now and always.

It is clear through the volume that we should not forget the lessons we have learned during the last two years about the importance of investing in infrastructure that can provide equal and sustained access to all participants (e.g., lending laptops and internet ports to those that cannot afford it at home; provide in-school/in-campus spaces for work), as well as support for teachers and students (e.g., in-school and out-of-school technical support; training; facilitating communities of practice). Most of the educators in the world suffered professionally and personally and came out of the crisis ready to keep learning and improving their teaching. This volume will help them accomplish it.

Finally, if this first volume of the new book series Developing Online Language Pedagogies is any reflection of the quality and creativity of the upcoming volumes, researchers, teachers, and teacher educators are in for a very special treat.

References

González-Lloret, M. (2020). Collaborative tasks for online language teaching. *Foreign Language Annals, 53*(2), 260–269. https://doi.org/10.1111/flan.12466

González-Lloret, M., Canals, L., & Pineda Hoyos, J. E. (2021). Role of technology in language teaching and learning amid the crisis generated by the COVID-19 pandemic. *Íkala, 26*(3), 477–482. https://doi.org/10.17533/udea.ikala.v26n3a01

Hodges, C., Moore, S., Lockee, B., Trust, T., & Bond, A. (2020). The difference between emergency remote teaching and online learning. [blog post] *Educause Review.* https://er.educause.edu/articles/2020/3/the-difference-between-emergency-remote-teaching-and-online-learning.

Mercer, S. (2021). An agenda for well-being in ELT: An ecological perspective. *ELT Journal, 75*(1), 14–21. https://doi.org/10.1093/elt/ccaa062

Mercer, S., & Gregersen, T. (2020). *Teacher wellbeing.* Oxford University Press.

Salmon, G. (2014). Learning innovation: A framework for transformation. *European Journal of Open , Distance and E-Learning, 17*(2), 219–1027. https://doi.org/10.2478/eurodl-2014-0031

Stickler, U. & Hampel, R. (2015). Transforming teaching: new skills for online language learning spaces. In R. Hampel & U. Stickler (Eds.), *Developing online language teaching: Research-based pedagogies and reflective practices.* Palgrave Macmillan.

1
Introduction

Ursula Stickler
Martina Emke

Introduction

As editors of the new Castledown book series Developing Online Language Pedagogies, we are delighted to present the first book in this series: Online language teaching: Crises and creativities. The idea for this book came out of the Covid-19 pandemic and of our observation, how different the reactions of language teaching experts to it were. While some researchers into technology and language learning immediately responded to the enforced move to online language teaching by setting up and conducting empirical research that traced the ongoing development, others reacted spontaneously with offers of help to fellow teachers with less experience or confidence in online teaching. In this tension between surveying and supporting, between crisis and creativity we located our own interest and decided to propose this book.

From early on in the pandemic, researchers published quick-shot questionnaire studies, classroom observations and literature reviews of language teaching as it was about to move online and language teachers' reactions. A random search on Google Scholar reveals more than 4000 articles published to the keywords Covid online "language teaching" in the year 2020. Some selected papers are referenced in this volume; however, this introduction will only look at examples of excellent practice in the drive to support language teachers; publications that we feel will stand the test of time and that were - at the time - a beacon to language teachers worldwide.

As the first of those, Julie Sykes edited a special issue of Foreign Language Annals in June 2020 (Sykes, 2020). Bringing together 16 articles by experts in the field, FLA supported teachers with immensely practical information about online community building, suitable tasks, and learner anxiety, as well as papers looking at evidence that online teaching works, and what makes for good collaboration.

Following closely, and showing the immense reactivity of teachers and publishers, McIntyre, Gregersen, and Mercer (2020) published their survey results on coping strategies during stressful times. The article helped to reassure language teachers that they were not alone in feeling overwhelmed and that there are different ways of coping with external stressors.

Another early study of how language teachers responded to the sudden move to teaching online in the wake of the Covid-19 pandemic comes from Gao and Xang (2020). The authors investigated Chinese language teachers' cognitions; the findings of this qualitative study indicate that the participants of this study adjusted their teaching remarkably well to the challenges associated with online teaching, based on their understanding of the learning needs of their students.

Published after more than two years of living through the ups and downs of the pandemic and associated restrictions and changes, this book takes a rather more long-term view. Focusing on Crises and Creativities (both in the plural), it allows us to take Covid-19 as one possible scenario of why and how the teaching of languages is changing and looking towards the future. Both short-term reactions and long-term impact of the rapid change in language teaching practice are being considered. As an edited volume, the book brings together experts from across the world who have in their own context and globally responded to the requirements of moving language teaching online. The contributors share the tension described above: a need to help in the short term combined with a desire to research what is going on to provide better and better-founded help in the future.

As editors, we believe that the trend towards an integration of more online teaching in face-to-face settings is irreversible, as is the demand for targeted (language) teacher preparation to enable effective teaching in this way. This development will certainly impact on teacher education programmes, which will need to be revised to accommodate the trend towards more online teaching.

Our own work has its foundation in socio-cultural theory, although in our individual works we have also explored the value of other theories for language education (Stickler, 2022; Emke, 2020). Since 2008, we have worked with language teachers and teacher trainers in experiential and dialogic workshops, reacting to their needs and starting points while sharing our views and expertise freely. We have discovered over the years that this approach is the most sustainable for us and for our students and participants. As researchers we acknowledge the co-researchers' or participants' voices as valuable and hope to present them in the published outputs of our work. As colleagues (whether in training workshops, teamwork, or research discussions) we listen to the expertise of others and value different perspectives. We believe that thinking together creates more valuable, more accessible, and longer lasting insights.

To allow our theoretical beliefs to come through in this work, as well, we designed a collaborative section: The final chapter of this book is a truly collaborative effort, allowing every author's voice to contribute their reasons for writing in their own style, their choice in helping and/or researching, and their visions for the future after the pandemic. We encourage other editors of books in this series to do the same. To bring together the different author voices in a dialogic format, and to give every contributor the chance to reflect and comment on their own and others' writing.

Apart from this introductory chapter, Online language teaching: Crises and creativities consists of seven chapters written by teams of authors or individual authors.

In Chapter 2, Pauline Ernest and Sarah Heiser provide an overview of reactions to the pandemic as and when it happened. They have collected articles published by researchers, questionnaires issued by educational institutions, and help-sites offered by public bodies. They find commonalities and different trends in how the world at large reacted to this specific challenge to move language teaching online quickly and thoroughly.

Chapter 3, written by an international team of Aline Germain-Rutherford and Banaf Karamifar from the University of Ottawa in Canada and Tomáš Klinka from the Charles University in Prague, Czech Republic, presents their respective institutions' provision for teachers and students in the rapid move online. They analyse questionnaires issued to staff and students over the course of more than a year, gauging changes in the reaction to online language teaching. Combining a framework of distance, presence, and proximity with elements of experiential and participatory learning, the authors develop a new approach for the design of online professional development workshops.

Chapter 4 is Jackie Robbins' and Joe Hopkins' account of how moving teacher training online in times of crisis has led to a re-design of small-scale training provisions into online video-streaming to thousands of teachers because of the massive immediate need. The way this one-to-many provision was still able to create real-time interactivity with participants is described in their chapter.

Chapter 5 relates another large-scale support activity: a toolkit created especially for language teachers at higher education institutions in the UK. Three of the creators of the toolkit, Karina von Lindeiner-Stráský, Elodie Vialleton, and Hélène Pulker, analysed data gathered from users to find out where the gaps in teachers' perceived skills were. This research links together the theoretical concept of the online language teaching skills pyramid with practical help offered to teachers in need.

Chapter 6, written by Sun Shin, goes deeper into teachers' needs and insecurities during the first months of the pandemic. Set in Korea, the author investigates teacher wellbeing and how the need to shift English teaching online has benefits as well as drawbacks. Data collected over a number of months, shows how the teachers' original hesitancy and doubts switch to a can-do attitude with some pride in their achievements. The theoretical framework for this study is based on the psychological concepts of stressors and coping strategies and enriches quantitative surveys conducted in this area with fine-grained qualitative data.

In Chapter 7, David Bish presents his concept of micro-blending. Of evident immediate use to teachers, the idea that pedagogic expertise is not lost when switching medium, is positioned within experiential data, and resulting in valuable suggestions to practitioners on how to make the most of their strengths while embracing change when necessary.

In the final chapter, Chapter 8, all authors contribute and reflect on their own work, on other chapters in the book, and on their position in the wider field of language teaching support during a pandemic. This chapter brings together the voices of all researchers and language teaching professionals involved in this book project. By setting up an asynchronous online debate, we were able to tap into the views of all our authors on the benefits and challenges of a move to online language teaching, enforced by crises, but - at the same time - unleashing unexpected creativities in dedicated, resilient, and enthusiastic language teachers and teacher trainers.

The new book series Developing Online Language Pedagogies covers different topics that are connected to online teaching and addresses a range of issues that are relevant to practitioners and researchers. This edited volume, the first in the new series, covers online language pedagogies from various perspectives: practitioners, experienced language teachers, and researchers of international reputation. As we hope that these viewpoints present the prospective readers of the book series, and that the volume will be of interest to language teachers, teacher trainers, language programme designers and educational researchers, we asked our authors to give us their views on what a book series like ours would ideally contain. To set the scene for this volume, to give you a taste of the final chapter and to outline our own views' with regard to this book series, we present the authors' responses here with our own reactions.

Question:

From your perspective as a language teaching practitioner / researcher, what are the advantages of a book series like Developing Online Language Pedagogies? What would you expect as a language teaching practitioner when you search for help using a book series or publisher's website?

Pauline Ernest:

I would hope to find reassurance that what I am doing as a practitioner / researcher is broadly in line with current trends and also be presented with new questions, concepts, research data etc which would lead me to re-examine and extend my current work.

Editors' response:

This was the gap in current educational publications that we identified:

Teachers / practitioners often find research publications too dense and sometimes irrelevant. We think that teachers benefit greatly from easy access to current trends and new research.

Aline Germain-Rutherford:

Any opportunity for language teachers to exchange teaching practices and experiences, academic perspectives, and realities from different parts of the world where they teach can only be enriching and formative. If the aims of the Developing Online Language Pedagogies book series are these, then I can only agree. I also dream of seeing multilingual publications of this kind.

Editors' response:

We are hoping that teachers will find the time and motivation to contribute to our series, and we are actively encouraging submissions directly out of practical experience. As editors it will be our responsibility to ensure the quality of the publications; however, we are not purists in terms of methodologies or academic style. And yes, publications in French, German, Spanish, Chinese… we can only dream that there will be a market for these in the future.

Joseph Hopkins:

I think the main advantage of the book series is that it aims to strengthen links between research and classroom practice, two aspects which unfortunately are often treated separately. In this respect, as a practitioner I would hope to discover innovative ways to enhance my teaching which have been validated by research findings.

Editors' response:

As teacher educators we sometimes find it hard work to convince teachers of the need to spend some of their valuable staff development time in reading theoretical articles rather than practising their skills on the latest tools. One of us is particularly keen on even linking highly theoretical concepts such as epistemology or knowledge frameworks to fundamental teacher training tasks, as the shifting realities of online environments make it crucial for teachers to understand how to best communicate with their learners online. We hope that the series will answer to these calls for supporting developing understanding and encourage all authors to speak to the classroom practitioner as well as to the curious researcher. We envisage the future contributions of our book series to become a solid bridge between theory and practice, research, and teaching.

Sun Shin:

I would expect to find different tools and practices I could adopt for online teaching. Also, knowing trends, concepts, and what other teachers have tried would broaden our horizons as teachers and help us to better deal with challenges in formatting our classes online.

Editors' response:

A part of what authors have presented as ideas for the series is exactly like that: immensely practical and applicable to the classroom. However, we do make sure that theoretical links do not get lost, and rather than training for the moment we would like to see what you describe in your second sentence: developing open-minded and confident online teachers through well-researched, well-presented, and immediately useful contributions.

Sarah Heiser:

I agree, examples of practice backed up with accessible, relevant, theory.

Editors' response:

Exactly so. The current volume is the first one to offer this mixture: some of the chapters look at more theoretical concepts, others focus on the help that is available and the help that is needed to make online language teaching sound and future-proof.

Hélène Pulker, Karina von Lindeiner-Stráský, and Elodie Vialleton:

Contributing to a book series like Developing Online Language Pedagogies gives the opportunity to come close to expert researchers in the field and showcase the Open University's work alongside recognised researchers in the field. It gives easy access to the latest research in the field by reading the other contributions and not having to search for them. Since the book is also directed at practitioners, we would hope to be able to disseminate our work among them and perhaps point them to new resources (such as our toolkit) and ideas. As language teaching practitioners we would expect to find practical guides and pragmatic teaching tips to improve online teaching, for example, the dos and don'ts. We would also expect publications that encourage reflection on our own teaching and practice. Perhaps also a few good references to the essential theories of teaching online.

Editors' response:

It is pleasing to see that there is a benefit for authors, as well. Of course, when we engage in research, we hope that it will further our own knowledge. However, we are aware that writing up your findings and presenting them in published form is hard work, and we are grateful to all contributors of this volume for the work they invested not only in their original support for language teachers but also now, in making their thoughts, ideas, findings and conclusions more widely available.

David Bish:

Teachers I have worked with are typically looking for advice and suggestions that they can apply readily; several chapters in this volume provide exactly that. They are looking for frameworks and techniques that reduce planning time and can be applied to make the next lesson go more smoothly. Teachers are looking for quick access to definitive reference material, rather than works that need to be fully digested before they can be applied. Teachers are still critical consumers of expert advice, however, and where something is contentious, unproven or subject to various interpretations I feel that this should be clearly indicated, allowing readers to relate the arguments to their own situation.

Editors' response:

An edited volume combines a variety of voices, and as such, we invite readers to select and react: we want them to tell us what works for them and what was most useful. And, like the concluding chapter to this book, we hope to foster real dialogue amongst expert practitioners through the book series and its readership.

Finally, we hope that the readers of this book will find the creative approaches described here valuable for their own teaching practice and research and invite them to send us their feedback, comments, and suggestions for future volumes in this book series.

References

Emke, M. (2020). Always In-between: Of rhizomes and assemblages in language teacher education research. In F. Bangou, M. Waterhouse & D. Fleming (Eds.), *Deterritorializing language, teaching, learning, and research: Deleuzo-Guattarian perspectives on second language education* (pp. 199–223). Brill. https://doi.org/10.1163/9789004420939_010

Gao, L. X. and Zhang, L. J. (2020). Teacher learning in difficult times: Examining foreign language teachers' cognitions About Online Teaching to Tide Over Covid-19. *Frontiers in Psychology, 11*, 549653. https://doi.org/10.3389/fpsyg.2020.549653

MacIntyre, P. D., Gregersen, T., & Mercer, S. (2020). Language teachers' coping strategies during the Covid-19 conversion to online teaching: Correlations with stress, wellbeing and negative emotions. *System, 94*, 102352. https://doi.org/10.1016/j.system.2020.102352

Stickler, U. (2022). *Technology and language teaching*. Cambridge University Press.

Sykes, J. (2020). Editor's message. *Foreign Language Annals 53*(2), 207–208. https://doi.org/10.1111/flan.12469

2
Teacher training in times of Covid-19

Pauline Ernest
Sarah Heiser

Introduction

As use of the internet has become normalised throughout society, many traditional educational institutions have moved to establishing VLEs (virtual learning environments) and integrating elements of internet-based tuition and learning resources into their professional development programmes for teachers. This has happened at a variety of paces, with the Covid-19 pandemic serving as an accelerator towards putting online learning into the mainstream.

This chapter will survey research prompted by a variety of educators' experiences during the period 2020–2021, when educational institutions worldwide were precipitately required to deliver at a distance. It will provide an overview of published reflections and teacher training options offered during the early months of the pandemic. There is difference and commonality. Each of the articles reviewed here reflects its own context and state of preparedness; all have shared their methods of adaptation to the unprecedented restrictions, with the aim of informing and learning from extremely challenging circumstances. In the second part of the chapter, we report on some published surveys of teacher reactions to Covid-19 and their training needs, and also present a selection of just-in-time guidance offered to language teachers during this period by national bodies and higher education institutions.

The language departments of two higher education distance learning providers, The Open University UK and the Universitat Oberta de Catalunya UOC, are of particular interest in the context of this chapter because, as well-established distance learning universities, academics at both institutions have consolidated experience in designing and facilitating remote learning. Both use synchronous and asynchronous online tools to support their students' language learning, the former having adopted blended learning, and the latter having been founded as an online university. And while this is their standard practice, it rapidly became a new, imposed and frequently improvised pattern of work for others during the pandemic. Both universities have established a strong tradition of professional development for teams of part-time associate lecturers, in order to bridge the gap between the teaching competence of these tutors in more traditional settings and the pedagogies of distance learning, and thereafter to help them keep up with the continuous changes in available technologies, which is standard in the online academic environment.

Established research on teacher development for delivery in online spaces shows the benefit of educators learning through a scaffolded experience, or experiential learning, which mirrors the type of delivery they will later use with their students (Ernest, Heiser, & Murphy, 2011; Salmon, 2011). Salmon's 5-step model (Salmon, 2002), in which mastering the basics of the technology is shown to be the necessary springboard towards using it for pedagogy, was first developed for forums but was equally applicable to synchronous online and blended delivery models. Specifically for language learning and based on research with part-time language teachers working in a distance teaching institution, a further model was developed which stepped the participant from establishing confidence in the online space through to developing a personal teacher style (Hampel and Stickler, 2005; 2015). Such models were created at a time when online learning was still largely the exception.

This chapter will review a dozen research articles and studies, published internationally in the first year of the pandemic, and available online either via open access or through a university library. The selection has both temporal and geographical aspects. Firstly, inclusion was due to timely availability, the result of prompt reflection and publication by the authors on the experience of taking their teaching online during extreme, unplanned circumstances. With the passage of time, their assumption of an imminent return to people meeting freely without fear of infection, becomes a snapshot of the point when the general expectation was that the pandemic would be solved by lockdown, and that lessons learnt about online teaching and learning would become elective, once again. Secondly, in order to reflect the global dimension, the selection was deliberately international, with some bias towards the UK, a reflection of author location and familiarity with that landscape.

International contexts

The first study takes us to Hong Kong. At the University of Hong Kong, the Initial Teacher Education programme for English language was suspended in February 2020 due to the pandemic. In a setting where students have an existing level of digital literacy and are preparing to become teachers themselves, discussion sessions, including micro-teaching activities, were transferred to video conference and when students were found to be reluctant to speak, preferring text-chat, adjustments were made. Break-out rooms were introduced to encourage students to interact more, and attendance became compulsory. The study notes the need for online skills development, preparedness of existing tutors and competences for online delivery to be included in the future training of its teachers (Moorhouse, 2020).

Surveying the situation in English, French, and German language teaching at Yarmouk University in Jordan, Alawawdeh and Alashtaiwi (2020) focus on 12 teachers and 38 students. Their data was gathered via questions, reflections, interviews and sharing of examples of instructional strategies, online tools, and student activity and they found that a mixture of synchronous and asynchronous practice had been adopted. They identified more systematic use of the university's e-learning platform, chat and messaging, for example WhatsApp, video conferencing (mainly Zoom), video streaming, for example YouTube, content making tools and online grading and assessment, but they also observe "that teachers have not yet given much consideration to the differences between traditional and online learning classes." (p. 10). Economic and environmental factors added to the challenges, with limitations on device ownership and internet connection, typical in rural and mountainous areas in Jordan. A further challenge was lack of student engagement, given their lack of prior experience of online learning, with a marked timidity to speak amongst those who attended Zoom sessions. The mention of these two challenges, in fact, reoccurs throughout these published reflections of 2020. In conclusion, the authors identify the need for preparation and planning, future educator training in technology-enhanced language learning and student digital literacy, with specific guidance for families with digital devices and secure internet connectivity being crucial.

Atmojo and Nugroho (2020), in Indonesia, elicited reflective writing from 16 EFL teachers from various cities, assembled through expression of interest, with some follow up interviews. The setting studied here is secondary schooling, where English is a subject valued for wider educational benefits and employability. From March 2020, all education went online, and teachers had to adapt to working from home and teaching fully online, with a minimum of prior experience "in a sudden and completely unprepared situation" (p. 52). Teachers were found to have used chat and messaging, video conferencing, video-streaming, and sharing, and content maker tools, for example the quiz-maker Kahoot, as well as online learning management systems and online libraries. There were environmental challenges, too: availability of devices, internet speed, parents "busy with their work and business" (p. 68) and health worries about excess screen time. The authors note that teachers "just move the face-to-face class into online learning environment" (p. 62) with no games, creativity, or innovation, and conclude that there is a training gap as the teachers did not have the experience to plan for asynchronous tasks to balance the synchronous sessions. The authors, thinking ahead, specify that in addition to mastery of the language they teach and language teaching pedagogy, future teachers require training in online language learning. They identify an investment need in internet provision and devices. Teachers, students, and parents need enhanced digital literacy and to "refine their misperceptions about online learning" (p. 65). And, in the short term, existing teachers require professional development in the knowledge and skills of online learning.

Also in Indonesia, Sugianto and Ulfah (2020) focus on the development of intercultural competences within English teaching, specifically the challenges and opportunities in times of Covid-19, via questionnaires and follow-up interviews with teachers, including some taking a Masters in English Education. Activities based on video clips and questions via readily available mobile device messaging at a university language centre and in a non-formal setting, such as private tuition, were reported to be received with enthusiasm and enhanced student criticality. Working with online texts, students found involving parents in online cultural projects and ease of feedback provision to be successful. Where innovation and creativity were reported, for example use of games and quizzes and students assessed partly through teacher observation of a WhatsApp discussion group, students were engaged and motivated. One success factor here was institutional support of online teaching and learning, such as training for video conferencing, peer observation of fellow teachers' Zoom sessions and effective teaching strategy development. While some teachers reported improved rapport with students and these taking more responsibility for their own learning, in general, the lack of social interaction and time spent online led to boredom and lack of engagement. The two standout challenges, again, were Internet access and student attitudes to the online classroom.

Faced with the same necessity to suddenly move online, teacher educators at the National University of Malaysia (Nasri et al., 2020) also identified internet coverage shortcomings in rural areas where some students on a pre-service language teacher training programme had returned because of the pandemic. This was partly mitigated by reliable advance publication of class schedules and use of communication tools that had mobile versions. Drawing on the expertise of an ICT lecturer, a help desk was established to support both "varying levels of ICT literacy amongst lecturers" (p. 4) and their students. "Just in time" training for staff was provided during the first two weeks of lockdown. Informed, inter alia, by a theory of online learning (Anderson, 2008), lecturers and student teachers, with their teaching practices also being forced online, were guided to design content mindful of student needs and teacher–student communication and to include feedback that was both synchronous and asynchronous. The authors conclude that future pre-service programmes should include instructional design not just for face-to-face settings but also for remote and online learning.

Moving to environments where internet coverage and device access are less problematic, Michigan State University, USA, reports that while the move to fully online delivery of courses in spring 2020 was sudden, it built on a decade of infrastructure and design in online language teaching (Gacs, Goertler, Spasova, 2020, p. 2). The required "just in - time training for teachers" (p. 4) is identified as needing to be short, impactful, fostering collaboration and requiring personnel for questions and support. Identification of learning objectives and affordances and limitations of online tools to be used, even briefly, is presented as high in utility (p. 6), with the desirability of online teachers learning through experiencing an online course (they reference Reinders & White, 2016), or, given the shortage of time, an in-house guide to successful online learning strategies (p. 9). They conclude that external circumstances have brought a "watershed moment" (p. 10) in online education.

The Transilvania University of Brasov, Romania already had a teaching platform in place for distance-learning programmes and "online tuition had already long been present in many universities, mostly as part of blended learning" (Maican & Cocorad, 2021, p. 2). While the emphasis of this article is on student experience, the benefits of developing teachers' transversal competencies in order to promote engagement with sustainable learning goals (UNESCO, 2017) is also identified.

At the Technische Universität Darmstadt in Germany, language instructors had, by a mixture of planning and good luck, six weeks to move their teaching online (Drucker & Fleischhauer, 2021). Staff with greater e-learning expertise supported others by offering workshops to train colleagues to facilitate synchronous online sessions. They shared theory, methods and techniques for synchronous and asynchronous online teaching and set up a virtual staff room with office hours for individual help. Given the changed situation, they produced an online netiquette guide for students. They also note the benefits for students of online collaborative language learning tasks (p. 182) and how instructors, previously divided by the language they teach, came together for cross-linguistic pedagogical exchanges (p. 185).

A similar ability to draw on theoretical grounding in times of need comes to light in two projects reported from Italy. When Italy went into lockdown as early as February 2020, the move to distance learning in Lombardy was born of necessity and "the teachers and institutions were not prepared for it" (Lo Presti, 2020, p. 91). Teachers of adult learners of Italian, for example, moved sessions to Skype and learnt "on the job." Assisted by existing literature on distance learning in languages, they found that materials sent in advance of sessions and teacher feedback were very well-received.

The post-graduate foreign language teacher trainer course at the

University of Urbino drew on the socio-constructivist Community of Inquiry framework, with a view to encouraging sharing and collaboration in knowledge building amongst students and developing reflection and critical thinking. Two-hour synchronous sessions and related asynchronous tasks were provided with published Learning Objectives (Carlon, 2020, p. 236). Carlon administered the Community of Inquiry questionnaire at the end of the course; it showed that students had been able to develop knowledge in their professional field, but that their experience of social presence or the sustaining feeling of human interaction with others could have been improved. In both Italian articles, the published reflection is presented as an important element, and as a step to post-pandemic course design.

UK context

The selection from the UK begins with two sector-wide commentaries, followed by further descriptive reports with their own reflections, each from a single university.

Paul Feldman, CEO of JISC, the UK Higher Education support organisation with an IT and digital resources focus, refers to the pandemic experience as "an inflection point in history, an opportunity for UK HEIs to build a better and stronger student digital experience" (Feldman, 2021, p. 45) in line with JISC's Education 4.0 vision. While celebrating the "amazing success" in March 2020 of the adjustments to fully move online (p. 39), he warns: "let us not kid ourselves that our disaster response represents a move to great online teaching" (p. 40). In fact, the term Emergency Remote Teaching (ERT) was coined in March 2020 (Hodges et al., 2020) in order to distinguish the precipitate, reactive move, as distinct from online or distance education course delivery, such as might be planned over a more normal preparation cycle of approximately six to nine months.

At Lancaster University the precipitate shift online led to a Covid-19 online teaching and learning community being set up to provide rapid-response support for staff (Munday, 2021). While much of the early function was considered to be "fire-fighting" (p. 64), it went on to become the digital education network for those prepared to embrace change (p. 68). It drew on established enthusiast engagement with digital teaching and learning of languages and applied it to the pandemic context (Stollhans, 2021, p. 107). Bristol University similarly provided academic staff with a week-long online course (Visintini, 2021, p. 58) which accelerated the "process of upskilling some colleagues in their use of technologies" (p. 61) with the existing VLE platform.

With a slightly longer lead-in time, the University of Oxford Language Centre took their existing team review meetings and staff development online, including lunchtime social time (Sadoux, 2021, p. 90). As early adopters of their new VLE, they were able to draw on existing relationships between learning technologists and teaching practitioners involved in course pilots, who themselves became peer mentors. Tutors were given a template to follow which included synchronous and asynchronous elements and was mindful of different language skills and varying broadband strengths. Despite many additional set-up hours being required, the resulting new agility and collaborative ways of working are identified as helping to build resilience (p. 94).

In February 2020, staff at the University of Southampton pre-sessional summer English Language programme (Borthwick, 2021, pp. 79–88), which caters for international students, became aware that there might be restrictions on taking entry tests and on travel. They therefore moved the programme online, using the synchronous and asynchronous tools offered by their current VLE. There was existing staff expertise, for example in designing MOOCs (Massive Open Online Courses), and an environment that allowed for welcoming and community building online. The University of Southampton is an example of an institution which offers an annual e-learning symposium and which rapidly moved online during the pandemic on the basis of existing experience of online language tuition. Given the uptake and efforts of the Covid-19 lockdown year, this will presumably be more common in the future.

The existence of faculty Digital Learning Directors (DLDs) and a centrally-based team of learning technologists at the university of Nottingham UK suggest an institution with some level of preparedness for going online. Here also, academics were offered training and were able to draw on dedicated support during the pandemic. Reporting that "a remarkable degree of pedagogical and technological creativity came to light" (Goria, 2021, p. 54), the author suggests that stereotypically change-resistant academics will adopt technology when they see the pedagogical value of doing so.

As the research above shows, there has been a vanguard engaged in online education going back some two decades. In the interim, with internet and mobile data access becoming more normalised there has also been a steady adoption of online learning and teaching in more traditional instructional settings as an add-on to the face-to-face classroom. Networking, typically online, and international teacher development projects (see https://ict-rev.ecml.at/ and Chapter 3 in the present collection) have brought together lone enthusiasts and helped improve confidence and competence in integrating online tools and opportunities into teaching practice and teacher training.

The sudden shift to remote learning in 2020 led to much reflection on the effects of this change, and on the elements authors anticipate they will integrate into their classroom practice in the presumed return to post-pandemic normality.

Feedback from surveys

A plethora of online training initiatives has been available to teachers during the pandemic. However, this has not guaranteed that teachers feel they have received sufficient support and professional guidance in transferring to full-time online delivery of their courses. Research on the challenges related to self-training and updating previously acquired skills is currently underway, with early indications suggesting that increased professional development opportunities are just one element identified as necessary by teachers. Several surveys have been undertaken and some are still ongoing. Given the unprecedented challenges experienced by teachers and teacher trainers worldwide at this time, it will be especially interesting to see how initial data gathered will contrast with future studies of this sort.

A survey by the EU School Education Gateway Online and distance learning (2021) was completed by over 5,000 teaching professionals. The following were the three main areas highlighted in response to survey question number four: "What would most help teachers to support online learning during the school closure?"

- More free resources and tools from Educational Technology Companies (44.6%)
- Clear Guidance from the Ministry of Education (41.4%)
- Professional Development: Quick courses on online teaching (37.4%)

Here, the need for more educational resources and clear guidelines from educational authorities appears to be more urgent than appropriate professional development related to online teaching. Similar conclusions are also emerging from a survey The future of language education. Learning lessons from the pandemic (2021) organised by the European Centre for Modern Languages (ECML) and completed by more than 4,000 teachers across Europe.

Initial results from both surveys indicate, however, that, once having managed to overcome initial challenges, a majority of teachers recognise the positive effects emerging from their pandemic-related professional experiences. For example, 55% of the ECML survey responses agreed, while 23% disagreed, with the following statement "We have been able to maintain the quality & variety of students/learners' language learning experiences and their achievements" (p. 24).

While both surveys highlight the need for an increase in professional development programmes, the ECML survey also includes some extremely negative comments:

> "It is an experience not worth living again. Teachers have gained more sources to work from, but they have been left without any professional help, which they could count on. Endless hours of personal work have been required to face the challenges of the pandemic" (p.

30).

This type of comment contrasts, nonetheless, with others. For example:

"It has given teachers a confidence boost since at the outset it was a daunting thought to have to teach online and now teachers are experts at it.... (p. 28). I have learnt the importance of the internet and online resources which I rarely used before. I have developed a lot of new skills" (p. 45).

Regarding assessment, while acknowledging that this can be an especially challenging area of online learning, 55% of ECML survey respondents agreed with the statement that "the replacement of tests and formal exams with continuous assessment overall, had a positive effect, especially in reducing stress" (p. 23).

The professional development section of the British Council site (https://www.teachingenglish.org.uk/article/support-teachers-teacher-educators) includes a report on three online surveys carried out by the British Council which examined the needs and experiences of teachers and teacher educators, and the role of Ministries of Education in providing support for primary and secondary educators during the pandemic. Survey results were presented at a webinar entitled Survey of teacher and teacher educator needs during the Covid-19 pandemic (2020). The almost 10,000 responses from educational professionals from over 150 countries emphasised the following needs (p. 4):

- More training and support in how to teach and how to train teachers online
- Clearer guidelines from Ministries of Education
- Identification of specific support resources needed by teachers
- Development of more resources for teaching online

Other areas of concern identified were class management, student motivation, assessment, poor/no internet connection, lack of appropriate equipment for teachers and students, inclusion of disadvantaged students, task design and student and teacher wellbeing. While confirming the findings of the two surveys mentioned above, the British Council survey also acknowledged that overall, the "ability to teach remotely was moderately high", and thus, alongside the need for clearer guidance from leadership, there was also "potential for knowledge sharing and peer support" (pp. 20–21).

This site also includes case studies of teachers and teacher educators worldwide who describe their positive experiences of overcoming pandemic related challenges, for example, Tuncel (2021). In addition, there are webinars on topics such as Teaching online: using your coursebook and ideas for breakout rooms (2020) and Teaching online: If the tech fails and structuring lessons (2020). Another topic identified here and less commonly found on similar sites, is an examination of how the pandemic has reshaped students' work experience and future career opportunities: Education exchange. Careers education in pandemic (2020).

A survey published by MacIntyre, Gregsen, and Mercer (2020), based on responses from 600 language teachers worldwide, explores the authors' previous work on the stresses and challenges to wellbeing of teachers when classes are required to rapidly transfer from a face to face to an online format. Factors identified include the blurring of the home–work boundary, frequently intensified when teachers are parents of school age children also in lockdown at home. The authors identify "an expectation that teachers will simply carry on and do their best by adapting, adjusting and continuing to aim for effective communicative language teaching using a range of online resources" with little in the way of preparation and training (p. 3), with insufficient institutional acknowledgement or maybe even awareness that "the skill set required for online teaching and developing courses that work well in the online environment takes time." (p. 9). They conclude that learning skills and strategies to "cope with the stress" (p. 12) should be included in pre-service and in-service teacher development.

Teacher training initiatives

We will now consider a selection of online training initiatives related to teachers' needs during the pandemic offered by organisations such as UNESCO, the European Commission and the European Centre for Modern Languages. Others have been provided by independent educational institutions, such as the UK Association for Learning Technology or the British Council/BBC, while others are in-house training materials shared by universities, such as the Massachusetts Institute of Technology and the University of Ottawa or specific open courses developed by the Universitat Oberta de Catalunya, and the Open University, UK.

Many of the above have tuned their guidance to the needs of teachers, who in some cases literally "overnight," were obliged to deliver their courses fully online due to the pandemic. Others have concentrated on extending content of already consolidated training courses, while also including a list of dos and don'ts aimed at teachers with little or often no previous training in delivering their classes online. It is interesting to note that in the survey organised by the School Education Gateway (see above) two thirds of the respondents stated that the closure of schools due to the Covid pandemic had led to their first ever experience in online teaching.

UNESCO's Covid distance learning solutions offers "a list of educational applications, platforms and resources... to help parents, teachers, schools and school administrators facilitate student learning" (p. 1). The organisation also highlights issues such as the provision of social care and interaction during periods of school closure and states that most of the items listed "offer functionalities across multiple categories" (p. 1). Thus, while offering an extensive list of resources such as learning systems for use on basic mobile phones, digital learning management systems, Massive Open Online Courses (MOOCs), self-directed learning content, collaboration platforms that support live-video communication, and tools for teachers to create digital learning content, it also provides information on psychosocial support and mental health issues related to the pandemic, with advice, for example, on how teachers, parents and caregivers should talk to children about Covid. A selection of texts written by distance education experts are especially pertinent here. These include Going online in a hurry: what to do and where to start (Miller, 2020); Advice to those about to teach online because of the coronavirus (Bates, 2020); The Covid-19 Online Pivot (Weller, 2020).

The European Centre for Modern Languages (https://www.ecml.at) offers a Treasure chest of resources for learners, parents and teachers in times of Covid-19 (2020). This includes a handbook/app for teachers and also for parents. Entitled The secret agent's handbook of language challenges, it offers a variety of fun challenges to help maintain learners' motivation during extended periods outside the physical language classroom.

In the section for teachers there are links to the webinars Take your language teaching online! Broadcast in May 2020 by members of the ICT-REV (Use of ICT in support of language teaching and learning) team, a project supported by ECML. Delivered in English, French and German with over 20,000 viewers, the webinar aimed to help teachers with little or no previous experience, who were suddenly obliged to take their teaching online (for more information, see Chapter 4). Alongside practical advice on pedagogical principles related to the use of technology in the classroom, the webinars showcased the ICT-REV Inventory of ICT tools and open educational resources (https://www.ict-rev.ecml.at), a repository of freely available online resources for language teaching.

The ECML website also includes information on a second technology-related project E-Lang. Digital literacy for the teaching and learning of languages. This project presents a pedagogical framework, based around "real-world' tasks" and modules for e-training in the use of digital tools and resources for language teaching and learning, with content relevant for teachers faced with pandemic-related challenges.

The Association for Learning Technology (https://www.alt.ac.uk/) has a section entitled Covid-19 Response and Support with details of online courses and conferences on moving teaching online. It also has a dedicated section, Online pivot, offering an extensive list of related articles, blog entries and links to initiatives offered by institutions worldwide, for example, Keep teaching, New York Institute of Technology; A 2020 going online guide, University of Windsor; CILT teaching online portal, University of Cape Town.

The professional development section of The British Council site provides a variety of professional development materials to support teachers during the pandemic including lesson plans, case studies, webinars, teaching tips, research articles and a Facebook Q&A support session. The provision of synchronous support for teachers and teacher educators, provided in real time, by a Facebook support group, is a strategy of particular interest, given the stresses of working online and from home, especially during a long period of confinement, and the risk of individual feelings of personal and/or professional isolation. This type of spontaneous, informal, synchronous support is less commonly found on similar sites.

Universities responded to the need for accelerated teacher training programmes during the pandemic with a range of online courses and resources offered both by institutions which had hitherto focussed primarily on a face-to-face educational model, and by those with a consolidated reputation offering only distance or online modes of delivery. While the former concentrated their efforts on providing guidance and training for their own faculty and instructors, albeit freely available to the public, the latter offered training programmes specifically tailored to a wider public.

The Massachusetts Institute of Technology (MIT), for example, created a website Teach remote containing resources, tools and guidance for staff suddenly obliged to teach remotely. Areas covered include establishing course goals and content, assessment, building a community of learners, student engagement, synchronous and asynchronous activities and accessibility and inclusivity.

The University of Ottawa offered a similar programme of support for its instructors via its Teaching and learning support service, with webinars, tutorials, lists of tools and resources, a Basic guide for transforming your course for distance learning, and also a variety of tutorials related to technology, such as how to use the university's virtual campus, and platforms such as Zoom or Microsoft Teams. The University of Ottawa also partnered with institutions such as the Université Laval, the Lebanese American University, Carleton University, Harvard University, University of Glasgow, among others, in the preparation of a white paper Disruption in and by centres for teaching and learning during the Covid-19 pandemic leading the future of higher education published by the International Observatory on the Societal Impacts of AI and Digital Technology (August 2021). This paper describes the challenges faced by higher education institutes since the start of the pandemic and the actions undertaken to deal with these, focussing on the ways that resources have been shared to support faculty and students during the transition to fully online courses.

The Universitat Oberta de Catalunya UOC responded to the pandemic outbreak with the inauguration of the Emergency Remote Teaching Programme (2020). Supplementing its initial and in-service training courses for all faculty, this programme targeted Spanish-speaking teachers unexpectedly precipitated into online delivery of their courses. Available worldwide and free of charge, it consisted of twenty-four training webinars offered live three times a week, and two MOOCs. Approximately 10,000 participants from 47 countries enrolled for the programme which covered topics such as design of online course, tools and resources for distance teaching and learning, collaboration in online learning environments and assessment and feedback. The UOC Centre for Modern Languages provided two of these webinars: Free Online tools for language teachers and Different modalities of written feedback: orientation and social presence. The UOC also published Resources for emergency teaching, a list of links to resources for online emergency teaching, similar to those offered by institutions mentioned above.

Similarly, the Open University (OU) UK responded to the pandemic by offering online training courses for teachers: a three-week online course How to teach online: Providing continuity for students was offered via the OU affiliate FutureLearn, covering areas such as creation of lesson plans, promotion of student engagement via interaction and the creation of an online community, assessment and feedback. In addition, the OU School of Languages and Applied Linguistics published a free online toolkit Moving your language teaching online (October 2020) which aimed to support language teachers from other Higher Education institutions with little or no experience in online teaching, suddenly forced to deliver their courses online (see Chapter 4). The Toolkit, which users are encouraged to modify, translate, and share with colleagues, consists of help sheets outlining the basic principles of online language teaching: creation of an online classroom; maintaining motivation and engagement and developing assessment strategies for online teaching and learning.

Conclusions

This chapter set out to survey reactions to the Covid-19 pandemic at various academic levels of language teaching and research. While the plethora of publications could not be covered in full, the authors identified four general trends in the ways language teachers, institutions and researchers responded to the enforced move to online teaching.

Firstly, there were the more or less traditional research studies (see above: International contexts) which investigate the effects of these changes via, for example, reflection and evaluation of teaching experiments capturing the reactions to the changes by teachers and students, and the gathering of qualitative data to contrast with pre-, and maybe post-pandemic evidence.

The second form of response can be found in the many descriptive reports undertaken at institutional or individual level to respond creatively to the enforced changes, for example by descriptions of staff development programmes, or by sharing examples of best practice (see UK context). These papers were of particular help to fellow language teachers if they were published as open educational resources (OERs) or in open educational practice (OEP) formats.

Thirdly, it was found that major international and transnational institutions invested their considerable reach to gather information on language teachers' immediate and longer-term needs (see above: Feedback from surveys). In contrast to the research-driven studies mentioned above, these surveys were presented more as a generic resource, with the aim of guiding institutions towards selecting the best possible support and resources for their staff (see above: Teacher training initiatives).

Finally, it became clear that many language teaching institutions reacted to the pandemic by offering free online training for those less proficient in teaching at a distance. And it was especially those institutions (see Teacher training initiatives) with a long track-record of distance language pedagogy who came to the aid of fellow teachers with courses, webinars, toolkits, and training materials provided as and when needed.

During the Covid-19 pandemic the challenges faced by all the stakeholders involved have been enormous: teachers, in particular, have needed to rapidly update existing skills and frequently also acquire totally new ones for online course delivery. They have been obliged to adapt content and methodology while thinking "on their feet," and simultaneously deal with professional and personal challenges related to their own well-being (see Chapter 6) as well as similar issues experienced by their students.

Future prospects

Despite the obvious challenges involved in the accelerated change to online teaching and learning, we hope that the findings outlined in this chapter will offer some early indications that there will also be lasting and positive results. In their concluding remarks, the authors of the ECML survey discussed above state that initial feedback from participants indicates an "equilibrium between the positives gained from the experience and the challenges to be faced' (p.25) and they are confident that 'this enormous work will not be lost and can be used in the future to improve teaching in general" (p. 47).

We also trust that the opening up of a range of possibilities for reflection, innovation and integration of new skills and resources and, above all, increased professional development opportunities, will remain as positive, long-term effects of the pandemic and as integrated elements of teachers' regular professional practice. The four different types of responses we describe: prompt research, reports of good practice, state-of-play surveys, and training and support initiatives, are four avenues that could be explored in more depth to prepare for future changes and challenges. All are important when considering how to ensure a successful transition to the integration of ICT in language teaching.

References

Anderson, T. (2008). *The theory and practice of online learning* (2nd ed.). AU Press.

Alawawdeh, N., & Alashtaiwi, M. (2020). Foreign languages e-learning: Challenges, obstacles and behaviours during COVID-19 pandemic in Jordan. *Palarch's Journal of Archaeology of Egypt/Egyptology 18*(6), 11536–11554.

Atmojo, A.E.P., & Nugroho, A. (2020). EFL classes must go online! Teaching activities and challenges during COVID-19 pandemic in Indonesia. *Register Journal, 13*(1), .49–76. https://doi.org/10.18326/rgt.v13i1.49-76

Borthwick, K. (2021). Complexity and simplicity during COVID-19: reflections on moving pre-sessional programmes online at pace. In A. Plutino, & E. Polisca, (Eds.), *Languages at work, competent multilinguals and the pedagogical challenges of COVID-19* (pp. 79–87). Research-publishing.net. https://doi.org/10.14705/rpnet.2021.49.1221

Carlon, G. (2020). Digital learning in foreign language teacher training in higher education: A case study. *Proceedings of ADVED 2020- 6th International Conference on Advances in Education.* https://www.ocerints.org/adved20_e-publication/papers/156.pdf

Drucker, D. J., & Fleischhauer, K. (2021). Language pedagogy in a pandemic: The shift to online instruction at a German university during the COVID-19 crisis. *Journal of Pedagogical Research, 5*(1), 172–187. https://doi.org/10.33902/JPR.2021167474

Ernest, P., Heiser, S., & Murphy, L. (2011). Developing teacher skills to support collaborative online language learning. *The Language Learning Journal, 41*(1), 37–54.

Gacs A., Goertler S., & Spasova, S. (2020). Planned online language education versus crisis - prompted online language teaching: Lessons for the future. *Foreign Language Annals, 53*(2), 380–392. https://doi.org/10.1111/flan.12460

Goria, C. (2021). Reflections on the impact of COVID-19 on teaching and learning in the Faculty of Arts at the University of Nottingham. In A. Plutino & E. Polisca (Eds.), *Languages at work, competent multilinguals and the pedagogical challenges of COVID-19* (pp. 47–55). Research-publishing.net. https://doi.org/10.14705/rpnet.2021.49.1217

Hampel, R., & Stickler, U. (2005). New skills for new classrooms: training tutors to teach languages online. *Computer Assisted Language Learning, 18*(4), 311–326.

Hodges, C., Moore, S., Lockee, B., Trust, T., & Bond, A. (2020). The difference between emergency remote teaching and online learning. *Educause Review*, (March 27, 2020). https://er.educause.edu/articles/2020/3/the-difference-between-emergency-remote-teaching-and-online-learning

MacIntyre, P. D., Gregersen, T., & Mercer, S. (2020). Language teachers' coping strategies during the Covid-19 conversion to online teaching: Correlations with stress, wellbeing and negative emotions. *System, 94*, 102352, https://doi.org/10.1016/j.system.2020.102352

Maican M.-A., & Cocoradă E. (2021). Online foreign language learning in higher education and its correlates during the COVID-19 pandemic. *Sustainability, 13*(2), 781. https://doi.org/10.3390/su13020781

Moorhouse, B. L. (2020). Adaptations to a face-to-face initial teacher education course "forced" online due to the COVID-19 pandemic. *Journal of Education for Teaching, 46:4*, 609–611. https://doi.org/10.1080/02607476.2020.1755205

Munday, Dale. (2021). Teaching and learning post pandemic. In A. Plutino, A., & E. Polisca (Eds.), *Languages at work, competent multilinguals and the pedagogical challenges of COVID-19* (pp. 63–69). Research-publishing.net. https://doi.org/10.14705/rpnet.2021.49.1219

Naffi, N., Davidson, A.-L., Snyder, D. M., Kaufman, R., Clark, R. E., Patino, A., Gbetoglo, E., Duponsel, N., Savoie, C., Beatty, B., Wallace, G., Fournel, I., & Ruby, I. (2020). *Whitepaper: Disruption in and by centres for teaching and learning during the COVID-19 pandemic leading the future of Higher Ed. Observatoire international sur les impacts sociétaux de l'IA et du numérique (OBVIA).* https://www.docdroid.com/L0khasC/whitepaper-disruption-in-and-by-centres-for-teaching-and-learning-during-the-Covid-19-pandemic-leading-the-future-of-higher-ed-21-08-2020-pdf

Nurfaradilla Mohamad N., Hazrati H., Siti Nur Diyana M., & Lilia H. (2020). Mitigating the COVID-19 pandemic: A snapshot from Malaysia into the coping strategies for pre-service teachers' education. *Journal of Education for Teaching, 46*(4), 546–553. https://doi.org/10.1080/02607476.2020.1802582

Presti, M. V. L. (2020). Second language distance learning: The issue of language certification in the time of COVID-19. *European Journal of Education, 3*(2), 1–16. https://doi.org/10.26417/755hnh40a

Reinders, H., & White, C. (2016). 20 years of autonomy and technology: How far have we come and where to next? *Language Learning & Technology, 20*(2), 143–154. http://dx.doi.org/10125/44466

Sadoux, M. (2021). How to flip it... never again? Towards agile models of work. In A. Plutino, & E. Polisca (Eds.), *Languages at work, competent multilinguals and the pedagogical challenges of COVID-19* (pp. 89–95). Research-publishing.net. https://doi.org/10.14705/rpnet.2021.49.1222

Salmon, G. (2002). *E-tivities: The key to active online learning*. Kogan Page.

Salmon, G. (2011). *E-moderating: The key to teaching and learning online* (3rd ed.). Routledge.

Stickler, U., Hampel, R., & Emke, M. (2020). A developmental framework for online language teaching skills. *Australian Journal of Applied Linguistics, 3*(1), 133–151. https://doi.org/10.29140/ajal.v3n1.271

Stollhans, S. (2021). Studying languages in the times of COVID-19: reflections on the delivery of teaching and learning activities and the year abroad. In A. Plutino, & E. Polisca, (Eds.), *Languages at work, competent multilinguals and the pedagogical challenges of COVID-19* (pp. 105–111). Research-publishing.net. https://doi.org/10.14705/rpnet.2021.49.1224

Sugianto, A. & Ulfah, N. (2020). Construing the challenges and opportunities of intercultural language teaching amid Covid-19 pandemic: English teachers' voices. *Journal of English Language Teaching and Linguistics, 5*(3), 363–381. https://pdfs.semanticscholar.org/e6f7/0bff3449e3139fc7a97e1dc06b15a640fe14.pdf

Visintini, G. (2021). The "go digital" Bristol experience. In A. Plutino, & E. Polisca, (Eds.), *Languages at work, competent multilinguals and the pedagogical challenges of COVID-19* (pp. 57–62). Research-publishing.net. https://doi.org/10.14705/rpnet.2021.49.1218

White, C. (2008). Innovation and identity in distance language learning and teaching. *Innovation in Language Learning and Teaching, 1*(1), 97–110. https://doi.org/10.2167/illt45.0

Institutions

British Council

British Council (2020). *A survey of teacher and teacher educator needs during the Covid-19 pandemic*
https://www.teachingenglish.org.uk/sites/teacheng/files/Covid19-teacher-teacher-educator-survey.pdf

British Council (2020). *Education exchange*. Careers education in pandemic. https://www.teachingenglish.org.uk/article/education-exchange-careers-education-a-pandemic

British Council (2020). *Support for teachers and teacher educators.* https://www.teachingenglish.org.uk/article/support-teachers-teacher-educators

British Council (2020). *Teaching online: if the tech fails and structuring lessons.* https://www.teachingenglish.org.uk/article/teaching-online-if-tech-fails-structuring-lessons

British Council (2020). *Teaching online: using your coursebook and ideas for breakout rooms.*
https://www.teachingenglish.org.uk/article/teaching-online-using-your-coursebook-ideas-breakout-rooms

University of Cape Town

University of Cape Town (n.d.) *CILT teaching online portal.*
http://www.cilt.uct.ac.za/teaching-online-portal

European Centre for Modern Languages (ECML)

ECML (n.d.) *E-Lang. Digital literacy for the teaching and learning of languages.*
  https://www.ecml.at/ECML-Programme/Programme2016-2019/Digitalliteracy/tabid/1797/language/en-GB/Default.aspx

ECML (n.d.) *ICT-REV Inventory of ICT tools and open educational resources.*
  https://www.ecml.at/ECML-Programme/Programme2012-2015/ICT-REVDOTS/ICT/tabid/1906/Default.aspx

ECML (2020). *The future of language education. Learning lessons from the pandemic.*
  https://www.ecml.at/Portals/1/documents/events/webinar-presentation-future-language-education.pdf

ECML (2020). *Treasure chest of resources for learners, parents and teachers in times of Covid 19.*
  https://www.ecml.at/Resources/TreasureChestofResources/tabid/4397/language/en-GB/Default.aspx

ECML (2020, May 6). *Taking your teaching online! A webinar for Language teachers.*
  https://www.youtube.com/watch?v=1Lt1gqzMBv0

ECML (2020, May 8). *Auf in die Online-Lehre! Ein Webinar für Sprachenlehrende* (Webinar)
  https://www.youtube.com/watch?v=vCDi4Uh9MFE

ECML (2020, May 11). *Passez à l'enseignement des langues en ligne ! Un webinaire pour les enseignants de langues* (Webinar)
  https://www.youtube.com/watch?v=ZrM13-eqonE

European Commission & EU School Education Gateway

EU School Education Gateway. (2021). *Online and distance learning.*
  https://www.schooleducationgateway.eu/en/pub/viewpoints/surveys/survey-on-online-teaching.htm

European Commission. (n.d.) *Education and training response/ Coronavirus learning resources: online platforms.*
  https://education.ec.europa.eu/resources-and-tools/coronavirus-online-learning

Massachusetts Institute of Technology (MIT)

http://teachremote.mit.edu/

New York Institute of Technology Keep Teaching

https://www.nyit.edu/ctl/keep_teaching

Open University UK

Open University UK. (2020). *Moving your language teaching online.*
  https://www.open.edu/openlearncreate/pluginfile.php/525015/mod_resource/content/2/Toolkit-version1-final.pdf

Open University UK. (2021). *How can you take your teaching online?*

https://www.open.edu/openlearn/education-development/learning/how-can-you-take-your-teaching-online

Open University UK. (n.d.). *How To teach online: Providing continuity for students*.
https://www.futurelearn.com/courses/teach-online

Open University UK. (n.d.). *Online teaching: Evaluating and improving courses*.
https://www.futurelearn.com/microcredentials/online-teaching-improving-and-evaluating-courses

Universitat Oberta de Catalunya UOC

Hopkins, J., Robbins, J. (2020, May 25). *Free Online Tools for Language teachers* (Webinar) Universitat Oberta de Catalunya.
https://www.youtube.com/watch?v=uU4orNTLGUA

Fernandez Michels, P. (2020, May 22). *Different modalities of written feedback: orientation and social presence*. (Webinar) Universitat Oberta de Catalunya.
https://www.youtube.com/watch?v=bXMI-9wl6yw

Resources for emergency teaching. Universitat Oberta de Catalunya
http://biblioteca.uoc.edu/en/resources/emergency-teaching

University of Ottawa

University of Ottawa (2020). *Disruption in and by centres for teaching and learning during the Covid 19 pandemic leading the future of higher education*.
https://observatoire-ia.ulaval.ca/en/whitepaper-leading-the-future-of-higher-ed/International

Observatory on the Societal Impacts of AI and Digital Technology
https://observatoire-ia.ulaval.ca/en/

University of Ottawa. Teaching and Learning Support Service (TLSS).
https://uottawa.saea-tlss.ca/en/teaching-continuity?idU=1

UNESCO

UNESCO Covid 19 distance learning solutions
https://en.unesco.org/Covid19/educationresponse/solutions

Rieckmann, M., Mindt, L., Gardiner, S., Leicht, A., Heiss, J. Education for Sustainable Development Goals: Learning Objectives. UNESCO. 2017 https://developmenteducation.ie/resource/education-sustainable-development-goals-learning-objectives/

University Council of Modern Languages

Online resource sharing
https://university-council-modern-languages.org/languages-education/online-resource-sharing/ (Accessed April 2021)

University of Windsor

Going online guide
https://www.uwindsor.ca/education/openpage

Other

Bates, T. (2020). *Advice to those about to teach online because of the coronavirus.* https://www.tonybates.ca/2020/03/09/advice-to-those-about-to-teach-online-because-of-the-corona-virus/

Miller, M. D. (2020). *Going online in a hurry: what to do and where to start.* https://www.chronicle.com/article/going-online-in-a-hurry-what-to-do-and-where-to-start/

Tuncel, C. (2021). https://www.teachingenglish.org.uk/article/Covid-19-case-studies-cigdem-tuncel

Weller. M. (2020). *The Covid-19 online pivot.* https://blogs.lse.ac.uk/impactofsocialsciences/2020/03/13/the-Covid-19-online-pivot-the-student-perspective/

3
Creating presence in remote learning: Moving a participatory f2f workshop concept online

Aline Germain-Rutherford
Banafsheh Karamifar
Tomáš Klinka

Introduction

This chapter aims to provide a comparative perspective of the abrupt migration to online teaching prompted by the pandemic in two institutions: The University of Ottawa, Canada, and the Charles University in Prague, Czech Republic. The authors, members of these two institutions, worked together following a pre-Covid-19 training course on technology-based education organised by the European Centre for Modern Languages (ECML/CELV) and offered to language instructors in Prague. The chapter discusses how the rapid transition from face-to-face to online teaching and learning modalities in the context of the pandemic provides an opportunity to reflect and rethink the teaching and learning paradigm.

In the Canadian context and with the emergence of communication technologies, the search for new forms of pedagogical support for post-secondary distance education was initiated in the 1990s (Power, 2002), but their implementation did not occur at the same pace in all institutions depending on their specific cultures and technological facilities (Power, 2002; Duplàa, 2011, 2012). However, in 2020, the pandemic challenged all institutions to rapidly transform to online or hybrid facilities. Surveys of academic faculty and administrators at Canadian higher education institutions conducted by the Canadian Digital Learning Research Association (CDLRA) in the spring and fall of 2020 highlight the significant impact the pandemic will have on higher education in terms of a sustainable transition to online teaching and learning (Johnson, 2020a).

A similar situation can be found in the Czech Republic in the context of higher education. Distance education, which was often considered to be inferior in quality and complementary to face-to-face education, only began to be officially supported by the Czech Ministry of Education in 2020 in the context of continuing education. However, the pandemic has created a need for new forms of education (e.g., distance or hybrid models of education) and this effort is now part of the third pillar of the official Czech state programme of "post-Covid renewal," funded by a substantial budget. Focusing on education and the labour market, this pillar proposes curricular changes and innovations in the context of digitalisation (Ministry of Industry and Trade, n.d.).

In the urgency to rapidly implement a distance education system, many institutions have had to address the gaps between this new reality and existing resources. Thus, in the Canadian context, the CDLRA 2020 report identifies several key elements, directly related to faculty professional development issues, such as:

> The need to increase faculty development programmes for teaching online, with a focus on facilitating student engagement, equity and access.
> A change with regards to the positive attitude that faculties have developed towards online teaching and an interest in using more technologies in their practices to offer agile and sustainable high quality online education.
> The need to find ways to provide students with virtual experiential learning opportunities (Johnson, 2020a & b).

Likewise, a series of surveys of academic faculty and students at the University of Ottawa during 2020–2021 echo the same conclusions regarding the need to strengthen faculty training in online technologies and course design to provide high quality online or blended learning experiences, improve student engagement, and increase opportunities for virtual experiential learning (University of Ottawa, 2021). Similar surveys at Charles University (2020, 2021) in Prague showed positive changes in the ability of teaching staff to meet the challenges of online teaching, such as lack of personal interaction, limited possibilities for substitution of practice-oriented topics, passive attitude of students or lack of feedback. Longitudinal surveys in both institutions show more positive indicators in 2021 compared to 2020, which demonstrates the universities' ability to cope with the new situation and adapt to this difficult context.

In both institutions the vast majority of students surveyed repeatedly during the academic year 2020-2021 cited their lack of motivation and the psychological pressure of isolation experienced during their online learning as major challenges (Charles University, 2021; University of Ottawa, 2021). Above all, the lack of socialisation during and between courses, the lack of a sense of proximity between their peers and with their instructor, the need for human presence and the distance felt during online courses had a significant impact on students' mental health, as shown by some excerpts from students' comments:

> *"Mental health was a big issue. Sitting in front of a screen all day isn't healthy at all."*

> *"It's not fun being unable to attend classes in person. I miss the interactions and dynamics. Online learning felt very lonely and isolated."*

> *"I hope this is over soon. I'd like to be human again."* (University of Ottawa, 2021).

These reported needs of students for a more "human" online learning experience during the pandemic and post-pandemic period (University of Ottawa, 2021) extend the training needs identified by educators in pre-Covid research, such as task design, manipulation of learning management systems, and techno-pedagogical skills (Sharp, 2011; Germain-Rutherford & Ernest, 2015; Karamifar *et al.*, 2019). We believe that a better understanding and awareness by educators of the concepts of "distance," "proximity," and "presence" in an online environment can help through improving the design and learning activities of online programmes, and thus the quality of the student learning experience.

In this chapter, after a brief overview of relevant literature, we will present and discuss the results of a series of surveys conducted with Canadian instructors on distance education during the pandemic. We will also report on the findings of a limited investigation on Canadian and Czech instructors' practices and perceptions about "distance", "presence," and "proximity" in online language education. Lastly, we will examine how these concepts apply to the design of online faculty development workshops, based on an experiential and participatory approach and on best practices recommended by scholars.

Part 1 Theoretical overview

The concepts of "distance," "proximity," and "presence" are key elements to consider in ensuring online learning environments of quality, and therefore have a considerable impact on the design and management of e-learning and pedagogical support. Taking these concepts into account can greatly improve student engagement, motivation and learning outcomes (Germain-Rutherford *et al.*, 2021). These concepts are discussed in the following paragraphs.

The concept of distance in online education

Distance in online education initially had a geographical meaning, indicating a lack of physical contact between teacher and students, as well as among students. "[It] identifies and describes teaching and learning that does not take place in classrooms, but in other places" (Moore & Marty, 2015, p. 1). In his theory of transactional distance, Moore (2015, 2018) questions the true nature of distance in online learning by adding to the concept of geographical distance the notions of pedagogical distance and of psychological distance. For Moore, the latter two types of distance, which are more a matter of pedagogical decisions and building supportive relationships to enhance learning, occur in both face-to-face and distance learning contexts and are therefore not solely due to the physical absence of the instructor in an asynchronous online environment. According to Moore, pedagogical and psychological distances have a greater impact than geographical distance on the quality of e-learning, particularly as geographical distance can be seen as more advantageous when learning becomes more accessible to a wider range of people.

Focusing more on pedagogical and psychological distances, Moore argues that they are at play not only in the delivery phase of an online course between instructor and learners, but also in the design of the online curriculum. Indeed, Moore's transactional theory of distance identifies three sets of macro-factors based on empirical research of curricula, teacher-learner communication patterns, and learner behaviour. The first macro-factor refers to the "structure" of the curriculum; the second relates to the level of "dialogue" between teachers and students, and the third reflects the degree of "autonomy" learners can achieve in deciding what they learn, how they learn it and how much they learn (Moore & Marty, 2015).

Structuring an e-learning course with the aim of creating an appropriate dynamic of dialogue between the learners, the learners and the teacher, and the subject matter itself, helps to reduce psychological distance and optimize learning. Dialogue is a key element in ensuring a positive and successful transactional distance on the basis of various criteria. Inherently constructive, "[d]ialogue is synergistic as each party in the exchange builds upon the comments of the other" (Moore, 1993, p. 26, cited in Moore, 2018, p. 35). The more psychological distance is reduced by organizing the online course in a way that promotes a high level of constructive interpersonal dialogue, the more space students have to take control of their learning and develop a high degree of autonomy (Dron & Anderson, 2014). This kind of autonomy is a significant change from the autonomy 'imposed' on learners in the pre-Internet and pre-Web 2.0 era, where geographical distance was the defining element of distance learning. Autonomy is now built into the pedagogical design of the course and enabled by the development of increasingly interactive and responsive technologies that allow for differentiated teaching and personalised learning.

The concept of proximity in online education

Spatial distance is the primary concern of educators who are used to teaching in a classroom, close to their students. However, with the development of digital technologies, the importance of physical presence and geographical distance in online education is becoming increasingly relative and the notion of distance is gaining in complexity (Paquelin, 2011).

Regardless of whether we are talking about teaching/learning face-to-face or at a geographical distance, the advances in information and communication technologies prompt us to think more about the concept of "appropriate distance", that is, "being situated neither too far nor too close to others, but in a space-time-social that delimits and contains the zone of participatory activities of the subjects that corresponds to what these actors are capable of achieving both individually and collectively to meet a need" (Paquelin, 2011, p. 566; translated from the French – own translation). Paquelin thus proposes to move from the paradigm of distance, "which separates," to that of proximity, "which connects" (Paquelin, 2011, p. 566). While validating a space of autonomy in which learners become aware of their personal capacities to carry out a project, they take the opportunity of the presence of others, including the coordination activities of the instructor. Hence, proximity is the result of a co-construction between the instructor's intention and the student's commitment and participation in learning activities, supported by technology. It is produced on one hand by situations of exchange in which the act of teaching and the participation of the students are embedded and on the other hand by common values that the instructor and the learner adhere to, beyond the geographical circumstances in which they are placed. Based on a Vygotskian perspective, Paquelin suggests an a-spatial proximity or organizational proximity which is divided first into resource proximity and coordination proximity and includes pedagogical strategies, such as sharing of the rules of operation of the system, establishing the regularity of participation in the workshops, communicating the nature of the productions to be made, the rules of exchange via the forum, and so forth. (see Paquelin, 2011, p. 575).

The concept of presence in online education

The concept of presence is added to the distance/proximity duality. It refers to a more concrete and more nuanced manifestation of an aspect of proximity: dialogue. Based on Moore's theory of transactional distance and on the importance given to the dialogue in reducing distance, Jézégou (2010, 2012, 2019) develops a theoretical model of 'presence' in e-learning, a key component for creating proximity in online environments: "In e-learning, presence contributes to reducing distance and generating proximity within a digital space of communication" (2019, p. 186; translated from the French – own translation).

According to Jézégou, presence is seen as "a relational dynamic" (2019, p. 194) related to the dialogue existing between the elements of a system. The feeling of presence is a representation of the relationship with others, based on affective feelings in distance learning. Thus, a loose structure, sustained dialogue, and social-emotional closeness through presence create a successful e-learning environment. Students' social presence, or "the ability of participants in a research community to project themselves socially and emotionally, in all dimensions of their personality, through the medium they use" (Garrison & Anderson, 2003, p. 55) is central to Jézégou's classification of presence and needs to be taken into account from the design and development of the e-environment to the management, action and running of the course.

In her model, Jézégou identifies three types of complementary social presence in e-learning: socio-cognitive, socio-affective, and pedagogical (2010, 2012). The first refers more to students and is generated by the transactions existing between learners to jointly carry out the activities necessary to resolve a problematic situation within a digital communication space. It is however supported by the socio-affective presence of students and instructors who interact in a constructive dialogue, which generates a positive and nurturing socio-affective climate favourable to learning. The pedagogical presence stems from specific forms of social interaction of coordination, moderation and facilitation that the instructor maintains with the learners (Jézégou, 2012, 2019). Jézégou (2019) points out: "The instructor's agentivity is essential to develop a pedagogical presence with the group of learners through the social interactions of coordination, facilitation and moderation that he/she maintains with this group. This presence is all the more useful as collaboration is not a practice that can be taken for granted, whether face-to-face or geographically distant." (p. 205, own translation).

Thus, the sense of presence within the digital communication space results from the combined effect of these three types of presence that together reduce distance, generate proximity and promote the emergence and development of an online learning community (Jézégou, 2012, 2019) despite the geographical distance between members of an online course. Furthermore, Jézégou's model draws on the principles of "adversarial collaboration" and "collective agentivity" from socio-cognitive conflict theory to fuel interpersonal transactions and further push the collective and individual co-construction of knowledge by students (Jézégou, 2019). In an online collaborative learning space where the confrontation of divergent viewpoints is valued and encouraged, students engage in concrete actions through mediated social interactions, comparing perspectives, exploring, and opting for new solutions.

Part 2 Instructors' perspectives

University of Ottawa survey results

Although phrased differently, these concepts of distance, proximity, and presence, and their centrality to a successful learning experience, are reflected in the many stories that students and instructors at the University of Ottawa shared during the pandemic, when they had to transition in less than a week, and with very little preparation and expertise, to online teaching and learning (University of Ottawa, 2021). In order to ensure that the accelerated instructors' training for online course design and development meets the needs and different levels of techno-pedagogical expertise of the instructors, and also that the courses thus developed provide students with a quality learning experience, the university decided to survey instructors and students three times during the 2020–2021 academic year. A longitudinal perspective would not only allow for further enhancing instructional support and monitoring the evolution of instructors' training needs, but also for improving the online experience of students over time.

To gain a better understanding of the transition experience, an initial survey was sent to 2,160 instructors in May 2020 garnering a 48% response rate. The second instructor survey was sent at the end of November 2020, garnering a 50% response rate, and the third was sent in early May 2021, obtaining a 47% response rate (University of Ottawa, 2021). In parallel, three surveys were sent to the students (University of Ottawa, 2021). The students repeatedly indicated that, overall, lack of motivation, the psychological strain of distance/isolated learning, and lack of face-to-face interaction with classmates were the most difficult experiences of online learning, followed closely by a lack of a sense of community or belonging and mental health difficulties. Psychological distance, and thus the perceived lack of presence of their peers and the instructor, remains prevalent. From the students' perspective, the notion of presence does not translate as an immediate physical proximity, it is the "sense of being in and belonging in a course and the ability to interact with other students and an instructor, although physical contact is not available" (Picciano, 2002, p. 22).

However, for the purpose of this chapter, which focuses more on instructors' training, we will primarily discuss instructors' responses to surveys, informed by students' feedback.

The first survey conducted at the beginning of the pandemic revealed that for 66% of instructors this transition to online teaching was their first experience of teaching in this modality. 62% of respondents then went on to indicate in the second survey that they felt ready to teach online in the following semester, thanks to the quick online training and support resources offered by the educational specialists at the university's Teaching and Learning Support Service. However, feedback received from students contradicted this optimism, voicing a strong sense that online learning modalities are less engaging, more difficult and less conducive to learning than traditional classroom courses. These results point to the need for greater diversity in pedagogical approaches and to the use of technology, encouraging greater interaction and relationship building.

While the responses to the three surveys show a progressive adaptation to the digital environment and to the geographical distance overall, other types of "distance" are expressed in the comments of teachers and students. One example is the technological distance felt by both instructors (the results of the first instructor survey underline, for example, the instructors' lack of expertise in identifying appropriate technologies for their courses and the need to learn how they work), and students (many students complained that instructors did not know how to use technology or did not use it properly). Another example is the pedagogical distance strongly felt by the students. Indeed, many instructors reproduced the lecture format in their online teaching, and students complained that the pedagogical design of their online courses left little or no room for interaction with their peers and with their instructor, and that active pedagogies were often absent (little or no group work, and very little use of collaborative technological tools). This created a great sense of isolation and a significant lack of motivation for most students in their studies.

However, findings of the third instructor survey indicate a 5–15% decrease in reported challenges as compared to the fall 2020 term, and a greater use of online technologies to increase active learning strategies and student engagement, such as tools to share materials, to interact with peers and instructors, and to work collaboratively on projects. With regards to resource or training related topics they would want to pursue, responding instructors shared that the greatest level of interest remains with supporting students' mental health and with learning more about strategies for engaging students in online learning. Finally, when asked what benefits from their online teaching experiences might carry over to future instructional contexts, several respondents mentioned the ability to be more creative in their teaching approaches:

"Being creative about delivering content, assignment design and engaging students. Thinking about teaching differently has helped me grow as a teacher."

"The variety in created content and approach may help support diversity in student needs. It supports creativity in an array of problem-solving circumstances."

These results are in line with the findings of the third parallel student survey, where 59% of students indicated that they felt prepared for online learning (a 15% increase from the first survey), with a higher level of engagement and ease of online learning. The integration of teacher-made videos, YouTube videos and collaborative editing tools such as Google Docs and Padlet, scored highest in terms of usefulness for learning. Compared to previous surveys, pair and group work increased in terms of reported use; as did the use of polls or brainstorming, student presentations, guest speakers and peer review. This indicates an increased use of more interactive and participatory teaching approaches. When asked what instructors had done that was most helpful in assisting them with the challenges of this past term, the psychological presence of instructors, through timely feedback and online availability, was often mentioned. Reducing distance, increasing the sense of presence to create proximity, was therefore at the heart of the concerns of both instructors and students.

Canadian and Czech Language instructors' perspectives

To find out more about the instructors' perspective in these times of change, we also surveyed a limited group of language teachers from Canada (n=11) and the Czech Republic (n=7) about their interpretation of the concepts of "dialogue," "distance," "presence," and "proximity" and how these concepts were reflected in their online teaching practice. Most of them were experienced language teachers (10+ years teaching experience) and their teaching contexts varied from secondary to post-secondary education.

Following the key concepts of Moore and Jézégou's theories, we first explored how instructors understand the notions of "dialogue," "distance," "presence," and "proximity" in the context of distance learning. For most of them, the term "dialogue" was associated with the notions of communication, exchange, sharing, participation, collaboration, and group work. Some also indicated that in the context of distance education, dialogue improved the quality of learning and opened up new possibilities. Another participant described their understanding of dialogue with three qualities: openness, structure, and flexibility. Concerns about the lower quality of dialogue during online courses were also raised by a few participants. When asked to name three concepts that lead to a successful dialogue between instructor and online learners, the first concept was, not surprisingly, again related to communication. Understanding, questioning, feedback, interaction or sharing were the most cited notions. The second cluster of concepts included positive values, such as clarity, openness, trust, patience, confidence, flexibility, or regularity. A third and final grouping was related to pedagogical themes, such as motivation, goals, team/group work, learner autonomy, teacher preparation or personal qualities of teachers.

When challenged to explain what distinguishes the three notions of distance, presence and proximity, the instructors expressed some difficulty in doing so. Again, they responded along three different axes. A group (four instructors) focused on the physical or technological dimension to explain the difference (absence or presence of cameras, use of certain tools, absence of physical contact). Another group, the largest (nine teachers), focused on psychological or pedagogical aspects, such as the level of activity, commitment, contribution, or even involvement of students, their participation in the course, and their interest in the courses. Three instructors emphasized the link between the three concepts:

> "Presence is very important because without it no learning can take place, distance and proximity follow."

> *"Presence and proximity are the favourable notions to not feel the distance."*

> *"I think that distance learning will not be distant as long as one is present with one's students."*

Finally, a small group (two instructors) focused on the positive aspects that these notions contribute to their teaching:

> *"These three notions have common aspects when it comes to teaching and learning online. While it is understood that with distance learning one has to be more disciplined in following the material received, following a face-to-face course also requires the learner to be proactive in learning. However, presence and proximity can invite the learner to take an active part in the sessions offered."*

> *"Distance is just in 'space', I take it as it is; presence depends a lot on the students, their motivation and involvement; proximity is a bit specific, but I personally try to be closer to the students in the online classes, I'm probably more personal than before."*

We also wanted to know if, and in which proportion (1-not at all, 5-always), instructors experienced, a sense of distance, presence and/or proximity while teaching online during the pandemic. Their answers, largely positioned between 3 and 4 for each concept, indicate that these notions were quite tangible. Three instructors report that they always had this feeling of distance, while two others always experienced a sense of proximity. Contrary to four others who said they never felt close at all to their students.

As for the impact of these concepts on their students' learning success, most agreed that more presence means more effective teaching/learning. However, three instructors noted that the concept of presence can be challenging:

> *"Distance allows flexibility (time, place); presence is much more difficult to maintain for both parties (technical problems, connection but also concentration, limited means of interaction); proximity being an essential aspect for successful learning."*

> *"In general, I find that presence is necessary for learning. For proximity, there are students who prefer to learn by themselves. Here, I think the impact would be more on social life."*

> *"Students were a bit reluctant to talk in front of the computer screen and get away from the teacher and others. However, they now feel closer since they started to open up, and they know that online teaching is our only solution to be connected."*

The results of this limited study show that while the factors of distance, presence, proximity, and dialogue are considered by this small group of language teachers to be important in the design and interactive dynamics of their online course, a deeper understanding and mastery of these concepts in order to implement them in their teaching practice would be beneficial.

Part 3 Distance, presence, and proximity in online teacher training

In this section, we will examine a concrete example in which a face-to-face language teacher professional development workshop concept was transformed into an online training during the pandemic without losing its experiential and participatory aspects, and while maintaining a high degree of presence, proximity and dialogue between facilitators and participants.

In the context of training in technology-integrated teaching and learning pedagogies for language education, a team of experts (including one of the authors) associated with the European Centre for Modern Languages (ECML) has been offering a series of training/consultancy workshops in the different member states of the Council of Europe for more than a decade (see Hampel & Stickler 2015 for a detailed description of the ECML's DOTS, MoreDOTS and ICT-REV projects related to this techno-pedagogy training).

The approach adopted by this team of experts in designing and facilitating the workshops is rooted in the teaching practice of the participating instructors and highlights the importance of the reflection process and the relevance of personal experiences in the acquisition of knowledge (see Stickler, Hampel, & Emke, 2020). As such, and as part of a lifelong professional development approach, the design and organisation of these workshops provide space for instructors to actively participate in creating their own pedagogical journey before, during and after each workshop. Based on participatory pedagogy (Askins, 2008; Siemens, 2008; Marta-Lazo et al., 2019) the workshops focus on experience, participation, and inter-creativity (a term that captures the strong relation between interactivity and creativity and thus the collective co-construction of knowledge, Marta-Lazo et al., 2019). During the workshops, participants share their professional background and experiences related to the use of technology in their classroom practices; they critically reflect on the opportunities and challenges of new media in teaching and learning languages, and collaborate in the creation of new learning activities using the most appropriate technologies to achieve particular pedagogical goals that can then be implemented in their own professional contexts (Ernest et al., 2019).

In the spring of 2021, the necessary transition to online professional development workshops as a result of the pandemic provided an opportunity for the team of experts to recreate the same level of inter-creativity

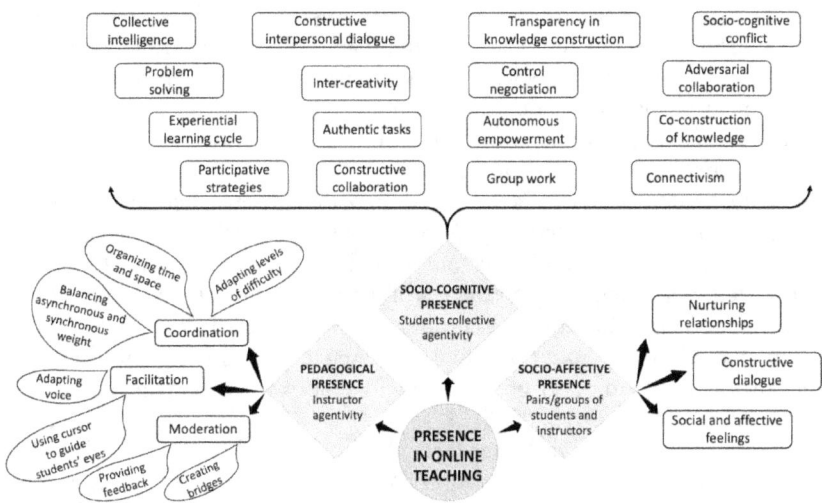

Figure 3.1 *Strategies for enhancing presence and proximity in online teaching*

and engagement of the language teachers participating in the training in an online environment. Adapting the spatial and temporal dimensions of the training to the new reality of online distance learning, the workshop sessions were spread over a week instead of the usual two intensive face-to-face days, alternating in a carefully balanced sequence between asynchronous interactions aimed at individual reflection and collective creation of pedagogical projects via the Microsoft Teams platform and chat rooms, and synchronous presence via videoconferencing dedicated to collective reflection, project presentations and sharing of experiences.

This rotation of synchronous and asynchronous presence and of individual and collective reflection has allowed the delimitation of a "proximal distance" (Paquelin, 2011, p. 567) that both connects and provides the distance necessary for a reflective process that enables participants to monitor their learning (p. 567). This "remote presence" (Peraya, 2011, p. 446) also allowed for the emergence of a rich dialogue in which converging or diverging ideas, strategies, pedagogical approaches and classroom practices were discussed, compared and negotiated, in a dynamic of "adversarial collaboration" as defined by Jézégou (2019) in order to come up with new and innovative solutions that could be implemented and tested in the particular contexts of the teacher-participants. The participatory and experiential space and dynamics of the training as reconstituted in the virtual environment thus made it possible to regain the socio-cognitive, socio-affective, and pedagogical dimensions constitutive of the e-learning presence (Jézégou, 2010, 2012, 2019), thus reducing distance and reinforcing proximity in order to privilege and facilitate quality online learning.

Based on Jézégou's model, Figure 3.1 presents the three defining dimensions of presence in e-learning (the diamond-shape), and a conceptual map of relevant pedagogical strategies and approaches from the literature (the rectangular-shape) that foster an online environment of dialogue, presence, proximity, and collaboration to support learners in their co-construction of knowledge and skills.

For instance, the socio-cognitive dimension of presence in an online environment is associated in Figure 3.1 with a number of pedagogical approaches and strategies such as a socio-cognitive conflict approach supported by participatory strategies of inter-creativity and adversarial yet constructive collaboration (Bandura, 1986; Marta-Lazo, 2019; Gil-Quintana, 2020) to build collective intelligence and thus promote cognitive problem solving and greater student empowerment (Jezegou, 2010, 2012, 2019; Moore, 2015, 2018).

In terms of pedagogical presence, the conceptual map highlights the search for a balance between enquiry and guidance, where the instructor needs to skillfully modulate their interventions as coordinator, facilitator and mediator to support and maintain the engagement and collaboration of distance learners, e.g. by adapting the level of difficulty when necessary, in their organisation of time and space, in their mediation of online dialogue, or even in their gestures and use of the cursor to guide students' eyes, thus enhancing their discourse with the visual (Jézégou, 2012, 2019; Tricot, 2017). But it is only by nurturing interpersonal relationships and social and affective bonds through constructive dialogues between students and instructors that a socio-affective presence can emerge (Bettoni *et al.*, 2007; Jézégou, 2010, 2012, 2019; Moore, 2015, 2018). Indissociable from the other two, this third dimension is essential to establish presence and proximity in e-learning, thus favouring "the emergence and development of an online learning community and consequently, the individual and collective construction of knowledge" (Jézégou, 2012, p. 3).

Conclusion

By prompting universities to make a sudden shift to online learning, the pandemic has accelerated a deeper reflection on the relevance of online education and the importance of better defining critical aspects of effective instructional design for online teaching and learning environments. Although distance education has a long history, the plight of the pandemic and the findings of several instructor and student surveys have shown that there is still a significant gap between distance education research findings, pedagogical practices, and teacher training to create online environments conducive to quality learning. Indeed, the studies discussed in this chapter show little familiarity on the part of instructors with active online pedagogies and limited use of educational technologies that promote online interpersonal and constructive dialogue, intercreativity and collaboration, or experiential learning. These findings are echoed by student surveys which report students' strong sense of isolation and their difficulty in coping with the lack of human presence and social interaction in their online learning, leading to low levels of motivation and disengagement in their studies.

We hope that the example of a concrete application of these concepts in an online participatory and experiential teacher professional development workshop presented in this chapter, as well as the conceptual map (Figure 3.1) based on Jézégou's model of presence in e-learning (Jézégou, 2012; 2019) can provide a useful framework to guide teacher trainers and instructors in the design of online and hybrid programmes that are caring, engaging, supportive, and conducive to a quality learning experience.

Our ideas for the future

An in-depth exploration of the concepts of "presence," "proximity," and "distance," and of the pedagogical strategies related to these concepts in order to create a "proximal distance" in a social space-time that delimits and contains a space of collaborative activities seem to be essential steps in professional development trainings aimed at instructors who teach in online environments.

Indeed, the increasing adoption of action-oriented, problem- and project-based approaches by language educators in recent years, together with the wider availability of interactive technologies and applications to promote active and collaborative online learning, can enhance the pedagogical, socio-cognitive and socio-affective dimensions of a sense of presence and belonging in an online language learning environment.

In a recent publication on lessons learned and post-Covid strategies for education, Wenmoth *et al.* have posed an important question: "How do we move the practice of instructional design to a level that embraces the student as a partner in the process of instructional planning?" (2021, p. 8). A promising direction for the future, in order to ensure not only behavioural but also cognitive and affective presence and engagement of students in their learning experience, is the increasing use of a design thinking approach (Gleason and Jaramillo Cherrez, 2021) in curriculum and instructional development to promote student agency.

> Learner agency is about having the power, combined with choices, to take meaningful action and see the result of those decisions. It can be thought of as a catalyst for change or transformation. Learner agency is about students having the understanding, ability and opportunity to be part of the learning design and taking action to intervene in the learning process to become effective lifelong learners. (Wenmoth *et al.*, 2021, p.4)

The professional development of language educators, with its emphasis on student agency and design thinking techniques in the conception of virtual environments and learning activities, will meaningfully engage students as responsible actors in their learning.

References

Askins, K. (2008). In and beyond the classroom: Research ethics and participatory pedagogies. *Area, 40*(4), 500–509.

Bandura, A. (1986). The explanatory and predictive scope of self-efficacy theory. *Journal of Social and Clinical Psychology*, 4(3), 359–373. https://doi.org/10.1521/jscp.1986.4.3.359

Bettoni, M. C, Andenmatten, S. & Mathieu, R. (2007). Knowledge cooperation in online communities: A duality of participation and cultivation, *The Electronic Journal of Knowledge Management, 5*(1), 1–6.

Charles University (2020). Distanční výuka na UK v období mimořádných opatření 2020 Studující/vyučující. RUK, UK. https://www.soc.cas.cz/aktualita/vysokoskolsti-studenti-behem-prvni-vlny-pandemie-koronaviru

Charles University (2021). Distanční výuka na UK v období zimního semestru 2020/21. RUK, UK.

Dron, J. & Anderson, T. (2014). *Teaching crowds: Learning and social media.* Athabasca University Press.

Duplàa, E., Sirota, T., Abdalla, N., Raymond, D., & Fodil, K. (2011). Institutional pedagogy and training of eTeachers: Engineering in Web2.0. Sùtra, The thread. *Quarterly Journal for Research on Education, Psychology, Traditional Sciences and Systems, Health and Consciousness*, 9, 123–144.

Duplàa, E. (2012). Approche institutionnelle et intégration des technologies dans l'enseignement supérieur. *Revue des Sciences de l'Éducation.* 37(2), 355–374.

Ernest, P., Hopkins, J., Emke, M., Germain-Rutherford, A., Heiser, S., Robbins, J., & Stickler, U. (2019). New media in language education. In D. Newby, F. Heyworth, & M. Cavalli (Eds.), *Changing contexts, evolving competences: 25 years of inspiring innovation in language education.* (pp. 89–99). European Center for Modern Languages, Council of Europe Publishing.

Garrison, D. R., & Anderson, T. (2003). *E-Learning in the 21st century: A framework for research and practice.* Routledge/Falmer. https://doi.org/10.4324/9780203166093

Germain-Rutherford, A., Davis, A., & Burrows, T. (2021). Effective student engagement strategies: A crucial alignment for sustainable, quality learning. *New Directions for Teaching and Learning*, 2021, 9–22. https://doi.org/10.1002/tl.20455

Germain-Rutherford, A., & Ernest, P. (2015). European language teachers and ICT: Experiences, expectations, and training needs. In R. Hampel & U. Stickler (Eds.), *Developing online language teaching: Research-based*

pedagogies and reflective practices (pp. 12–27). Palgrave Macmillan.
Gil Quintana, J., & Osuna-Acedo, S. (2020). Transmedia practices and collaborative strategies in informal learning of adolescents. *Social Sciences, 9*(6), 92. https://doi.org/10.3390/socsci9060092
Hampel, R., & Stickler, U. (Eds.). (2015). *Developing online language teaching: Research-based pedagogies and reflective practices. New language learning and teaching environments.* Palgrave Macmillan.
Jézégou, A. (2010). Créer de la présence à distance en e-learning: Cadre théorique, définition, et dimensions clés. *Distances et savoirs, 8*, 257–274.
Jézégou, A. (2012). La présence en e-learning: Modèle théorique et perspectives pour la recherche. *International Journal of E-Learning & Distance Education, 26*(1). http://ijede.ca/index.php/jde/article/view/777/1409
Jézégou, A. (2019). La distance, la proximité et la présence en e-Formation. In A. Jézégou (Ed.), *Traité de la e-Formation des adultes* (pp.143–163). De Boeck Université.
Johnson, N. (2020a). *Digital learning in Canadian higher education in 2020. National report.* Canadian Digital Learning Research Association. http://www.cdlra-acrfl.ca/wp-content/uploads/2021/05/2020_national_en.pdf
Johnson, N. (2020b). *Digital learning in Canadian higher education in 2020. Ontario report.* Digital Learning Research Association. http://www.cdlra-acrfl.ca/wp-content/uploads/2021/03/2020-regional_ontario_en.pdf
Karamifar, B., Germain-Rutherford, A., Heiser, S., Emke, M., Hopkins, J., Ernest, P., Stickler, U., & Hampel, R. (2019). Language teachers and their trajectories across technology-enhanced language teaching: Needs and beliefs of ESL/EFL teachers. *TESL Canada Journal, 36*(3), 55–81. https://doi.org/10.18806/tesl.v36i3.1321
Marta-Lazo, C., Frau-Meigs, D., & Osuna-Acedo, S. (2019). A collaborative digital pedagogy experience in the tMOOC "Step by Step." *Australasian Journal of Educational Technology, 35*, 111–127.
Ministry of Industry and Trade (n.d.). https://www.planobnovycr.cz/pilire#pilire
Moore, M. G. (1993). Theory of transactional distance. In D. Keegan (Ed.), *Theoretical principles of distance education* (pp. 22–29). Routledge.
Moore, M. G., & Marty, O. (2015). *La théorie de la distance transactionnelle.* halshs 00777034 https://halshs.archives-ouvertes.fr/halshs-00777034/document
Moore, M. G. (2018). The theory of transactional distance. In M. G. Moore (Ed.), *Handbook of distance education* (pp. 32-46). Routledge.
Paquelin. D. (2011). La distance: questions de proximités. *Distances et savoirs, Hermès Lavoisier, 9*(4), 565–590. https://www.cairn.info/revue-distances-et-savoirs-2011-4-page-565.htm
Peraya, D. (2011). Un regard sur la « distance », vue de la « présence ». *Distances et savoirs, 9*(3), 445–452. https://www.cairn.info/revue-distances-et-savoirs-2011-3-page-445.htm

Picciano, A. G. (2002). Beyond student perceptions interaction, presence and performance in an online course, *Online Learning, 6*(1), 21–40. https://doi.org/10.24059/olj.v6i1.1870

Power, M. (2002). Générations d'enseignement à distance, technologies éducatives et médiatisation de l'enseignement supérieur. *Revue de l'éducation à distance, 17*(2), 57–68.

Sharp, S. K. (2011). Teachers' acquisition of CALL expertise. *International Journal of Computer Assisted Language Learning and Teaching, 1*, 1–16.

Siemens, G. (2008). *Learning and knowing in networks: Changing roles for educators and designers.*https://www.semanticscholar.org/paper/Learning-and-knowing-in-networks%3A-Changing-roles-Siemens/7658e432ffc19798da8501bd2bee46123ea57618

Stickler, U., Hampel, R., & Emke, M. (2020). A developmental framework for online language teaching skills. *Australian Journal of Applied Linguistics, 3*(1), 133–151.

Tricot, A. (2017). *L'innovation pédagogique.* Éditions Retz.

University of Ottawa. (2021). *Transition to distance / online teaching and learning: Snapshot of instructors, students and teaching assistant experiences.* https://uottawa.saea-tlss.ca/en/survey-june-2020

4
Webinars as a rapid response for training language teachers to teach online in 2020

Jackie Robbins
Joseph Hopkins

Introduction

In this chapter, we reflect on the urgent need, brought on by the Covid-19 pandemic, for teacher development initiatives in the use of Information and Communication Technology (ICT) in language teaching. We then go on to the principal focus of this chapter, which is to describe how one series of webinars was conceptualised, developed, and delivered via YouTube Live as a rapid response to help meet this need. Following this, we present the results from a survey which was sent to attendees in order to evaluate the impact the webinars had on teaching practice during this challenging time. We conclude with some recommendations for future initiatives of this type of language teacher professional development.

The global health crisis brought on by the Covid-19 pandemic in 2020 had a huge impact on all those involved in education. The crisis struck when most educational institutions were still unprepared for the learning opportunities afforded by digital technologies. As Schleicher (2020) explains, while digitalisation can assist educators with teaching and testing, there is still work to be done to ensure that technology is integrated and will also "build a culture that facilitates learning, unlearning and relearning throughout life" (p. 5). Schleicher reports that despite the huge number of resources and tools which are readily available, educators continue to struggle with implementing them on a large scale while retaining high quality.

The issue of previous experience and appropriate training in online language teaching is not a new area of research in education. Meskill and Sadykova (2011) suggest that one key challenge for teachers when moving their teaching online is the shift to more learner-centredness. The teacher's role also changes from "provider of knowledge" to "facilitator of learning" (Bax, 2003), which involves careful design of tasks which are supported by technology. However, the overnight move to online contexts brought about by the Covid-19 situation meant there was "simply no time for anybody in education to prepare" (Appel & Robbins, 2021), and teachers often found themselves attempting to replicate their face-to-face classes in online formats. In a similar vein, Llanes warns that while pre-service training candidates often "have well developed digital skills and master the communication tools they use in their daily life, they have many difficulties when trying to integrate technology in the lessons they carry out at their host schools during their internships" (Llanes, 2019, p. 49).

With so many teachers being forced to make the shift to virtual teaching contexts so swiftly, in the spring of 2020 training became a key area of concern for many, not only in terms of preparation for working with specific tools and platforms, but also in terms of the pedagogical implications that this shift has. In this sense, Moser *et al.* (2020) present the results from a US survey into changes and perceptions of language teachers during the pandemic. They point out that numerous adjustments to previous procedures and policies were required and highlight the need for effective remote teaching which includes increased access to appropriate training in the use of technology. This study also notes the link between online instruction, remote teaching and pandemic-induced trauma; the authors find that teachers without prior experience were the "least confident that instructional goals were met despite having reported well-designed courses" (Moser *et al.*, 2020, p. 1). Highlighting one of the challenges in the move to online teaching, Littlejohn (2020) points out that prior to the pandemic, teachers were able to modify their teaching strategies in line with observed learner needs. This, however, became far more challenging in online contexts, particularly if the model failed to include direct interaction with learners. Littlejohn also identifies issues in the areas of student self-regulation and motivation, which often seemed to wane, and indeed, without direct interaction among teachers and learners, it was often difficult for teachers to help learners develop their self-perception as learners. Littlejohn concludes that more effort is required to allow for spontaneous connections, which are crucial for learning, because by default digital environments favour formal and planned interactions.

The disruption to traditional teaching caused by the pandemic did not only affect the mode in which teachers (and everyone) had to work. The health crisis also had an undoubtedly marked impact on stress levels. MacIntyre *et al.* (2020) examine the way in which teachers coped with a major world stress event, with or without prior experience or training. They report the results of a survey of 634 language teachers in April 2020. These authors find that the most frequently used coping strategies were acceptance, advanced planning, positive reframing, actively doing something about the situation, and using work as a distraction. These coping strategies, based on those identified in earlier work by Carver *et al.* (1989), are distinct from avoidant coping strategies. This draws on earlier work by Tran *et al.* (2017), who examine the emotional responses of university lecturers to a significant (and stress-inducing) change in research policy. Tran *et al.* identify four principal responses: enthusiastic accommodators, who embrace change; pressured supporters, who reluctantly go along with change; losing heart followers, who lose faith in the system over time; and discontented performers, who oppose change openly. The study shows that it is the lecturers' beliefs and goals which determine their emotional response to change, and not their career stage, qualification, or area of specialisation. Similarly, Appel and Robbins (2021) examined the emotional well-being of language teachers with prior experience in online teaching during the early stages of the pandemic as they move part of their normal face-to-face teaching online, too. The findings in this study show that prior experience of online contexts seems to lead to increased levels of confidence in implementing ICT into other educational contexts. Appel and Robbins report that most teachers in their study seemed to deal with the uncertainty of the pandemic in an emotionally positive way, but they also point out that in addition to pre- and in-service professional development, a strong support system is essential for the successful implementation of online learning.

In sum, in the early days of the pandemic, teaching and learning was transferred to online contexts from one day to the next, often with little or no training in the tools available or in how to utilize them in a pedagogically sound way. Prior experience and, especially, confidence seem to play a major role in how teachers adapt to stressful changes in the context of incorporating ICT into language teaching. The urgent need for training early in the pandemic was evident to all; however, many institutions were not in a position to provide this. For those that were prepared for training, there remained the question of the format in which to deliver the information to as many people as possible. In the following sections, we shall describe how the various people involved in ICT-REV, a Training and Consultancy initiative of the European Centre for Modern Languages (ECML), worked together to help meet this challenge.

The ICT-REV Project

ICT-REV has its origins in two previous projects sponsored by the ECML, namely, DOTS (Developing Online Teaching Skills; 2008–2011) and moreDOTS (2012–2013). Beginning in 2013, the main goal of the ICT-REV team is to provide language teaching professionals in Europe with training in the effective use of technology in their teaching. Up until March 2020 this training consisted of face-to-face workshops lasting over two days. One of the principal outcomes of the project, which is one of the main focal points in the workshops, is the ICT-REV Inventory of tools and open educational resources (https://www.ecml.at/ict). The inventory consists of a list of online tools and applications proposed by language teachers who may or may not have attended the workshops. Each tool is evaluated by the team members in terms of four criteria: firstly, the added value the tool offers for achieving learning objectives; second its usability; thirdly, its interactivity and the possibilities the tool offers for learners to communicate and collaborate; and fourthly, the key technical requirements.

The ICT-REV team members all have extensive experience working online; five out of the seven team members work in distance learning universities that rely heavily on technology and all members of the ICT-REV team have been giving face-to-face workshops on the use of technology in language teaching and learning in countries around Europe and beyond for many years (for more details, see Ernest *et al.*, 2019; Stanojević, 2015; Stickler, Hampel & Emke, 2020). These workshops, which are led by two or three of the project team members, are guided by the principle that effective teacher professional development programmes should emulate and model the underlying beliefs about what meaningful learning is. They are composed of three interrelated phases: pre-workshop, when participants answer an online survey and take part in an online activity; the workshop itself; and post-workshop, when participants are encouraged to develop a community of practice (Stickler, Hampel, & Emke, 2020). Karppinen (2005) argues that for learning to be meaningful, it should be a) active, b) constructive and individual, c) collaborative and conversational, d) contextual, e) guided and f) emotionally involving and motivating. These concepts are also related to the construct of learner engagement, whereby for learning to be most successful, there needs to be behavioural, cognitive, and emotional engagement. In other words, while information can be made available, learners need to be active participants, they need to think about what they are learning, as well as have an emotional connection to that learning in order for it to become meaningful (Robbins, 2020).

Figure 4.1 shows how the face-to-face part of a typical ICT-REV workshop unfolds, following these four main stages: 1) community building and reflection, 2) input/expansion of knowledge, 3) application of knowledge and collaborative design of a learning activity using ICT, and finally 4) community consolidation and cascading.

Conceptualising, planning and delivering rapid-response webinars

At the end of March 2020, the ICT-REV team met online to discuss future workshops and also to share impressions of the Covid-19 situation. During our meeting, the idea emerged of offering an online version of our workshop. We considered the possibility of offering a small session

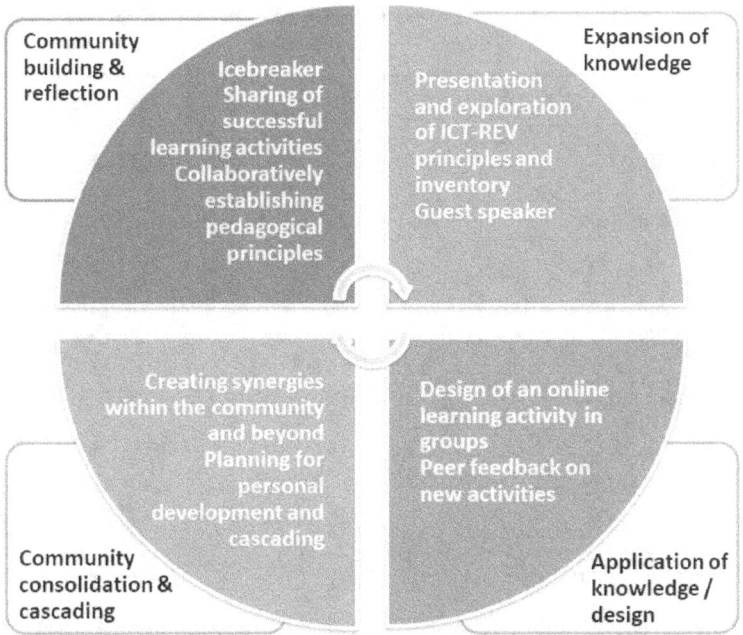

Figure 4.1 *The ICT-REV workshop cycle*

with similar numbers to our face-to-face events (around 25 participants) and repeating this for different groups of teachers of different languages in different time zones. We were confident we could provide a useful training opportunity for some teachers to help them adapt to the ever-worsening situation.

The team approached the ECML to establish whether they would be able to host and advertise an online event through the ECML network. Their enthusiastic response motivated us to push forward, and the event began to take shape. In recent years, our team has given abridged conference versions of our two-day training event and this enabled us to take key decisions regarding the contents of the online event: our primary aim was to introduce participants to and demonstrate the use of our freely available tools inventory without omitting the crucial element of the pedagogical factors which need to be borne in mind when choosing tools for specific teaching purposes.

As regards the platform for our event, we were all familiar with synchronous video conferencing tools such as Skype, Google Meet and Microsoft Teams and we were beginning to discover, along with many in 2020, the potential of Zoom and Jitsi. Time constraints meant that we

Table 4.1 *Top ten responses to the question "What types of digital functions/tools would be most useful in your teaching context now?" (N = 1578)*

Tool type	Responses	Percentage
Quiz maker	649	41.13%
Game app	517	32.76%
Audio record/edit/share	430	27.25%
Question/answer management	405	25.67%
File sharing/syncing	401	25.41%
Crossword puzzle creator	399	25.29%
Videoconferencing	363	23.00%
Story creation	360	22.81%
Video record/edit/share	326	20.66%
Course management	310	19.65%

would be able to offer a training event of 90-120 minutes for 30 or 40 participants, so that we could ensure interaction between presenters and participants and among one another in small groups. We also believed it would be best to have at least two team members leading the online workshop, as we do in the face-to-face workshops. However, the week before the first event, we learned that more than 1500 people had registered. In light of the huge amount of interest, the ECML proposed we offer a YouTube Live broadcast instead of a closed Zoom meeting. In this way, we would be able to reach a larger number of teachers, but of course, many of the interactive parts of our session needed to be rethought. We decided to make use of the multilingual nature of the ICT-REV team and therefore decided to offer three two-hour webinars: one in English, one in French and another in German. In total, over 4,000 people signed up for one of the three webinars, 2,738 people participated live (1,759 in English, 502 in French, and 477 in German), and at the time of writing, the videos have been viewed over 20,000 times. For each webinar, we had two facilitators, with the rest of the team members carrying out the role of moderators in the YouTube Live chat, together with several of our colleagues from the ECML. Technical support was provided by the ICT specialist and a trainee at the ECML.

Write an adjective which best describes your experience of teaching languages fully online.

Figure 4.2 *Results from Mentimeter asking participants to describe their experience of teaching languages fully online*

For our face-to-face workshops, we generally send an extensive survey to the participants several weeks prior to the event. The responses provide us with a clear idea of the participants' profiles in terms of languages and levels taught, familiarity with and attitudes to ICT, as well as a background for participants' views of pedagogical approaches to language teaching. This information helps us to tailor the contents of our workshops to the participants' specific needs. For the webinars, however, our aim was to provide support to teachers as quickly as possible. Thus, there was no time to administer and analyze the results of a comprehensive survey sent to more than 4,000 potential participants. We therefore sent a link to a very brief survey to the teachers who had registered for the online events in order to guide us in the selection of content. Specifically, we asked each of them to select three types of online tools they would be interested in exploring during the sessions from a list of 30 options (see Table 4.1). At the end of this short questionnaire, we also asked participants to provide us with their email addresses if they agreed we could contact them after the webinars for a follow-up survey. A total of 1,578 people responded, with 928 giving their consent to receive the post-event survey.

In spite of the constraints regarding interactivity implicit in a massive live online event and the lack of much previous knowledge about the audience, our goal was to a) involve our participants in real time as much as possible in order to increase engagement, and b) have an indication of their previous experience using technology in their language teaching. We therefore adopted several strategies to create a dialogue with the participants. The first of these was a Mentimeter activity (https://www.mentimeter.com/) which we presented during the first part of the

Figure 4.3 *Word cloud presenting results from previous workshops in answer to the question about difficulties using ICT in language teaching*

webinar. Using this tool, we were able to ask participants to write words to describe their previous experience and this was shown in realtime during the webinar in a word cloud format. Figure 4.2 shows the word cloud from the English webinar in response to the question "Write an adjective which best describes your experience of teaching languages fully online."

Figure 4.2 shows that, out of the 1,863 responses to this interactive instant polling tool, one of the most common words participants used to describe their experience of teaching online was "challenging" but we can also note other terms teachers wrote, such as "interesting" and "stressful". In a very real sense, these seemed to confirm the need for our webinars. It should be noted that the number of responses is higher to the actual number of participants in the live session (1,759) since viewers of the recording were still able to respond to the poll.

We also wanted participants to feel part of the community of language teachers in a practical way, or in other words, to let them know that they were not alone. One use of the survey results for our face-to-face training events is to identify difficulties teachers are facing when teaching with ICT: for example, lack of familiarity with appropriate tools, training, or criteria for selecting technology. We therefore revised information from our previous workshops and selected several pieces of data to present during the webinar. One of these was a word cloud which highlighted the need for online teaching tools (see Figure 4.3); this idea provided us with

Robbins & Hopkins   53

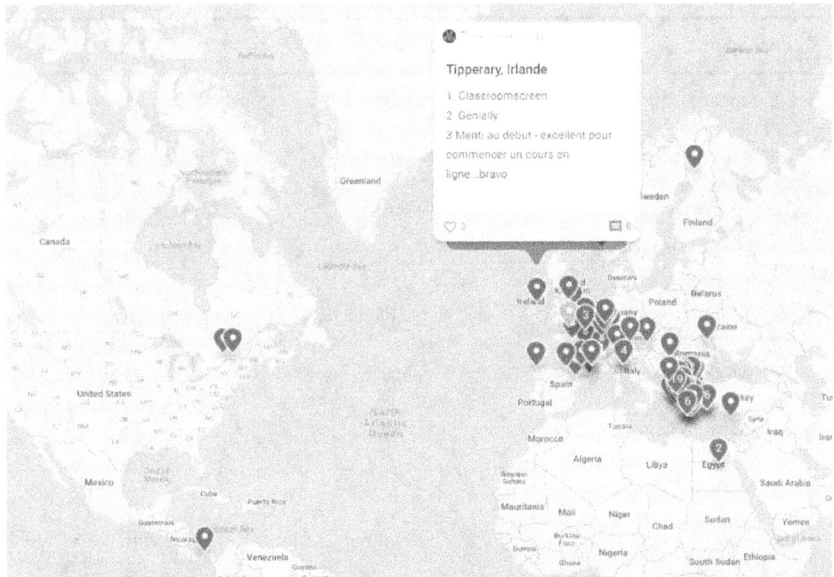

Figure 4.4 *Screenshot of Padlet used in the French webinar where participants were asked to add a post in their location noting three things they would take away from the webinar*

a natural introduction to the primary aim for the webinar, sharing the ICT-REV inventory.

Another strategy we used to interact with the webinar participants was with Padlet (https://padlet.com/). We asked participants to add a post to an interactive map which showed their location and add notes about three things they would take away from the webinar. Figure 4.4 shows the results from this activity.

As displayed in Figure 4.4, participants were mainly based in Europe. This is not surprising, given that the ECML network spans 35 countries in Europe and Canada. Figure 4.4 also shows that participants used the option to refer to some of the tools they had seen in the webinar.

We have already established that a crucial objective of the online event was to showcase several tools in our inventory, not only in terms of how they worked, but also how they could be used with students for specific learning objectives and activities. Each pair of webinar hosts selected examples of specific tools based on the types identified as most useful by participants in the pre-event survey (see Table 4.1). Our aim was to ensure that over the series of webinars we demonstrated a range of tools. Table 4.2 shows the tools presented in one of the webinars.

A range of tools with different types of functions was selected. We selected several quiz/game apps, a tool for recording audio and a video-

Table 4.2 *Tools presented in the English webinar*

Tool type	Examples	
Quiz maker	Mentimeter	Socrative
Game app	Kahoot!	Akinator
Audio record/edit/share	Audacity	Vocaroo
Question/answer management	Moodle	Google Classroom
File sharing/syncing	Google Drive	Dropbox
Crossword puzzle creator	EclipseCrossword	LearningApps
Videoconferencing	Skype	Zoom
Story creation	Storymaker	Book Creator
Video record/edit/share	Screencast-O-Matic	Voicethread
Course management	Moodle	Google Classroom

conference tool. In addition, we also referred to tools for course management and video recording. This selection was based on the survey responses and our conversations with teachers at our respective universities and prior experience with teachers new to working in online contexts in previous ICT-REV workshops.

Another key feature of our face-to-face training is to encourage participants to explore the inventory for themselves. To emulate this in the webinar format, we incorporated a break during which participants could do the same. We also used this break period to achieve another aim of the webinar: to allow us to interact with the participants and offer responses to their questions and comments in the YouTube Live chat. To this end, our colleagues who were moderating the chat throughout the session copied questions and comments from participants onto a shared Google Doc, which we then focused on in the final part of the webinar. Given the high number of comments and questions, the moderators curated these to avoid repetition and sorted them into categories.

In sum, as can be seen on Table 4.3, the rapid-response webinars were designed and delivered following as much as possible the general stages in an ICT-REV face-to-face workshop adapted to a YouTube Live webinar format (cf. Figure 4.1). There were, of course, severe limitations in terms of the amount of community building possible due to lack of time, the large number of participants, along with the fact that they could not see one another and only interact with one another via the chat. Like-

Table 4.3 *Relationship between the activities in the webinars and the stages in face-to-face ICT-REV workshops*

ICT-REV face-to-face workshop stages	Activities in the YouTube Live webinars
Self-reflection, community building & reflection	Pre-workshop survey; Participants shared feelings about moving teaching online in Mentimeter and posted questions and comments to the moderated chat.
Input/Expansion of knowledge	Presentation of the ICT-REV Inventory of tools
	Q & A via chat - questions answered by presenters
Applying knowledge/design	Not covered due to time constraints.
Community consolidation & reflection	Padlet activity: Participants indicated where they were on an interactive map and wrote 3 things they would take away from the webinar.

wise, it was not possible to have participants apply new knowledge by designing a learning activity in small groups, as we usually do in the two-day face-to-face workshops.

Survey to participants

Three months after the three webinars had taken place, a survey was sent to the 928 people who had given their consent to be contacted again to find out about the impact the experience had had on them. In this survey, participants were asked closed and open questions about their use of the inventory since the webinar and the effect this had had on their teaching. We also asked them about their subsequent use of any tools. In addition, participants were asked about their confidence in using technology in their teaching before, immediately after and three months after the webinar in August. 135 of the 928 (14.5%) responded. The response rate was relatively low, most likely due, in part, to the following factors: 1) not all of the people who had given their consent to be contacted had actually attended the webinars, 2) the questionnaire was not sent immediately after the event, but rather after three months had passed, and 3) it was sent in August, when many of the participants were on summer break. Nevertheless, the results do provide us with some insight into the participants' perceptions regarding the usefulness of the sessions.

Through the survey we sought to find answers to the following questions:

How much did the participants make use of the content presented in the webinars?

How did the webinars affect the participants' perceived level of confidence in using technology in language teaching?

Survey results

In this section the most relevant findings are presented from the survey sent out to the attendees of the webinars.

Figure 4.5 shows responses in answer to the question of whether participants had used the inventory since the webinar. There was an approximately 50:50 split between participants who said they had and had not used the inventory since the webinar.

We also asked participants how often they had used the inventory since the webinar and to describe any positive effects this had had. Figure 4.6 shows the results from the participants who had used the inventory after the webinars and as we can see, most reported that they had made use of the inventory once or twice, but 19 have used the inventory up to five times with 14 participants saying they had used it between five and ten times.

We performed a content analysis of the 56 comments in response to the question about the positive effects the inventory had had. The most frequently occurring theme (38 comments) was how teachers used the inventory: principally, responses were in relation to the discovery and use of new tools (17 comments) and creating more fun, motivating, and engaging lessons (17 comments). For example, one participant wrote "I could plan more interesting and amusing activities for my students." The second most frequently occurring theme (22 comments) in the responses to this question were descriptions of the inventory: these either referred to the ease of use of the inventory (e.g., "informative", "handy," and "inspiring"), or how the inventory saved teachers time (mentioned seven times). As one respondent wrote, "Having this inventory has saved me a lot of time in searching for online tools." Four of the comments referred to a specific learner profile (3 comments referred to young learners and 1 comment referred to training teachers).

Given that we had selected specific tools to present during each of the webinars, we also asked participants to indicate whether they had used these tools in particular. Figure 4.7 shows the results and as we can observe, approximately half of the participants reported that they had.

When asked which tools they had used, the most commonly mentioned were Mentimeter (mentioned 17 times), Kahoot (mentioned 11 times), LearningApps, Quizlet and Zoom (each mentioned nine times), as well as over forty other applications. Respondents did not elaborate on how they had used these tools.

A central theme for our questionnaire was to find out whether at-

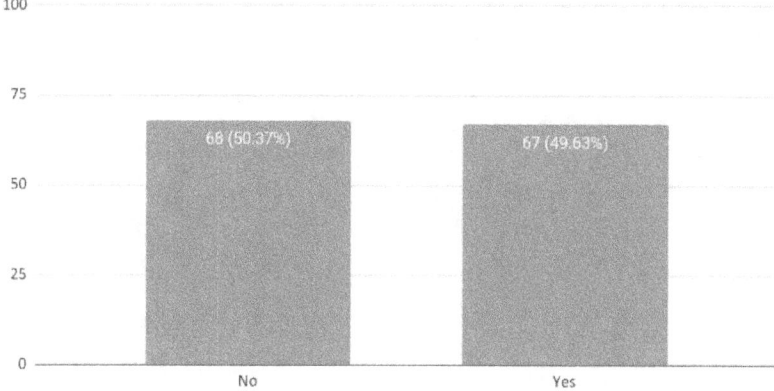

Figure 4.5 *Responses to "Have you used the ICT-REV inventory since the webinar?"*

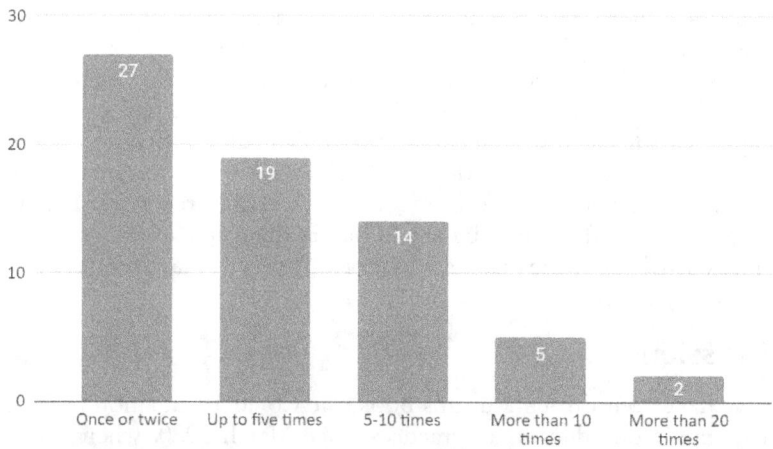

Figure 4.6 *Responses to "How often have you used the ICT-REV inventory since the webinar?"*

tendees felt that their level of confidence in using ICT had changed after the webinar. Participants were asked to rate their level of confidence from 1 to 10 before the webinar, immediately after, and "now" (i.e., when they filled out the questionnaire). Table 4.4 shows the mean and standard deviation results for these questions. As we can observe, the levels of perceived confidence increased from before the webinar to im-

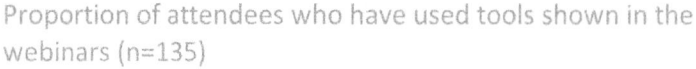

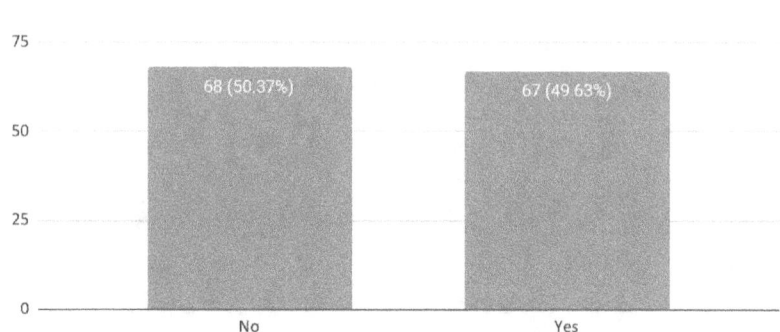

Figure 4.7 *Responses to "Have you used any tools you saw in the webinar?"*

mediately after the webinar, and then again to when they answered the questionnaire.

Table 4.4 shows that the mean levels of perceived confidence showed the largest increase from before to immediately after the webinars. There was also a slight increase from immediately after the webinars to "now" (three months after the webinars). We also carried out a *t*-test analysis to determine whether there was a significant difference between the means. These results are displayed in Table 4.5. The findings confirm a significant increase in perceived confidence in all three cases: 1) before vs. immediately after the webinars, 2) before the webinars vs. "now" and 3) immediately after the webinars vs. "now," with the largest effect found for cases 1) and 2).

Discussion

As we have seen throughout this book, the Covid-19 situation has had a huge impact on educational practices since March 2020, when teachers around the world were forced to move their classes online with minimal or even no time to prepare. The online education carried out during the early days of the pandemic in many institutions became known as 'emergency remote teaching' (Hodges *et al.*, 2020) and thanks to its implementation, a large proportion of students have had the chance to continue their education despite a lack of forward planning. In this context, many institutions essentially replicated traditional classroom-based teaching practices through synchronous classes and were initially not able to adapt their pedagogical practices to meet this radical change. A range of training courses, webinars, and tutorials appeared quite early on in the

Table 4.4 *Mean level of confidence before the webinar, immediately after, and now*

	Before the Webinar	Immediately after the Webinar	Now
Mean	6.09	7.70	7.94
N	129	129	129
Std. Deviation	2.073	1.589	1.435

Table 4.5 *Results of paired samples t-tests*

	Paired Differences								
				95% Confidence Interval of the Difference					
	Mean	Std. Dev.	Std. Error Mean	Lower	Upper	t	df	Sig. (2-tailed)	Cohen's d
Before vs. immediately after	-1.612	1.188	0.105	-1.819	-1.405	-15.417	128	0.000	0.871 (large effect)
Before vs. now	-1.853	1.537	0.135	-2.120	-1.585	-13.695	128	0.000	1.038 (large effect)
Immediately after vs. now	-0.240	0.864	0.076	-0.391	-0.090	-3.159	128	0.002	0.159 (small effect)

pandemic and one of these initiatives emerged from the ECML, specifically with the webinars offered by the ICT-REV team.

In the previous sections, we have described how a two-day face-to-face teacher development course was adapted so that it could a) take place in a webinar format, b) take place in 120 minutes and c) retain the key element of engagement and active participation by attendees despite being delivered via a medium which is largely unidirectional (presenters to attendees). The overall aims of the webinars were to present the ICT-REV inventory and provide language teachers with a tool which could be of immediate practical use in their daily work, to boost their confidence in the incorporation of ICT into their teaching and, in so doing, to support their overall emotional wellbeing during a global crisis (Appel & Robbins, 2021). At the same time, in the careful planning of the webinars, we strove to retain as much as possible a participant-centred approach, which is a hallmark of our face-to-face workshops and which has been highlighted as one of the key challenges of teaching online (Bax, 2003;

Meskill & Sadykova, 2011). We feel these aims were largely achieved, despite the pedagogic concessions we were forced to make due to time constraints and the large number of participants.

The training model discussed in Stickler *et al.* (2020) assumes a clear three-stage timeframe for workshops and ideally, the condensed webinars would have followed the same cycle. However, as can be seen from the questionnaire responses, the pre-questionnaire was much briefer and did not invite deep self-reflection that we could draw on during the sessions. It did, however, provide us with indications about the types of tools teachers were most interested in learning about and this helped us prepare the contents of the webinars. Regarding interactivity, during the webinars we encouraged participants to connect with the presenters and one another in the chat area in YouTube Live. The webinar moderators answered questions and responded to comments there, but the presenters were also able to give participants a voice as the comments and questions they contributed became the content of the final stage of the webinar. Likewise, the use of the applications Mentimeter and Padlet also allowed participants to express themselves and to be listened to. All these features helped to create a less unidirectional webinar format and fostered participants' emotional engagement with the event (Robbins, 2020). On another note, we as presenters found that the immediate feedback received—the participants' voice—helped greatly to put us at ease when addressing a massive and otherwise faceless audience.

In the post-webinar survey, we sought to find out how much the participants made use of the content of the webinars. From the results we have seen in the previous section, at least half of the respondents appeared to have found the content of the webinars useful and the numerical results are supported by the responses to the open-ended questions in the questionnaire. These findings seem to indicate that the content of the webinars was appropriate for our audience, at least at the particular time the webinars took place. This in part is thanks to what we learned in the pre-event questionnaire. Time constraints meant that we had to be selective, but we were able to demonstrate the types of tools most commonly identified as being of interest to the participants. We also wanted to know how the webinars affected our participants' perceived level of confidence in using technology in language teaching. The results we have presented appear to indicate that the webinars were offered at the right time for teachers' needs, as respondents perceived their confidence to have increased from before the webinars to immediately afterwards, and again when they responded to the questionnaire three months later. As Appel and Robbins (2021) argue, teachers' confidence in the use of technology is a contributing factor to the emotional wellbeing of teachers. One should bear in mind, however, that responses came from a mere 135 of the 2,738 participants total attending the webinars, thereby rendering any claims of generalizability tentative, at best. As mentioned previously, this could be in part due to the length of time between the live events and the sending of the questionnaire (three months) and the moment when it was actually sent (during many teachers' summer break). We would therefore recommend that similar issues of timing be avoided in order to increase response rates.

Conclusions

As this chapter set out to show, webinars as a rapid response to teachers' needs in an emergency situation are a practical way to offer help and support to teachers. We were able to adapt our model swiftly and effectively to a very large-scale event that retained some of the central elements of our regular workshops by showcasing the ICT-REV inventory, encouraging the participants to explore this and by incorporating tools which enabled participants to take an active part in the webinars. Our two main constraints in adapting to a webinar format were time and mode of delivery. Despite these limitations, we were able to foster interaction, and as a result, increase behavioural and emotional engagement (Robbins, 2020) of the webinar attendees. This, ultimately, appears to have boosted their confidence in using ICT in their teaching.

Recommendations for future online training

Reflecting on the experience overall, we have learned that the following elements are key to a successful interactive online training event via YouTube Live:

> Dedicated technical support to organise the session and to be available in case of any technical difficulties.

> Careful selection of interactive tools (e.g., instant polling, instant word clouds, virtual pinboards) to increase engagement amongst the participants.

> Colleagues in the session in order to moderate the chat and to relay selected questions to the presenters for them to comment on.

In addition to the above, we would also recommend having more than one presenter. In this way, participants have the opportunity to listen to more than one voice and the delivery is less unidirectional, more conversational, and potentially more engaging, as opposed to a one-presenter format.

As mentioned previously, unlike in our face-to-face workshops, we were unable to achieve much in terms of community building or to provide participants with the opportunity to apply newly gained knowledge together with fellow teachers. This was simply not possible due to the urgency of the situation. However, with time and careful forward planning, similar large-scale online training events could be offered and then complemented with smaller follow-up events organised at the local level, either online or face to face. Equipped with the appropriate training activities, the aim of these events could be to foster a sense of community and collaboration amongst specific groups of teachers (e.g., teachers at a particular school, school district, etc.) and to provide them with the opportunity to explore together, put into practice what they have learned in the webinar and learn from one another.

The experience described in this chapter shows, on the one hand, that it is possible for experienced (online) trainers to rapidly and effectively move their professional development sessions online to address immediate needs. In the long term, however, more resources should be allocated to this type of training, regardless of emergency needs, to maximise its impact.

References

Appel, C., & Robbins, J. (2021) Language teaching in times of Covid-19: the emotional rollercoaster of lockdown. In, Chen, J. (Ed.) *Emergency remote teaching: Voices from world language teachers and researchers.* Springer.

Bax, S. (2003). CALL—past, present and future. *System, 31*(1), 13–28. https://doi.org/10.1016/S0346-251X(02)00071-4

Carver, C. S., Scheier, M. F., & Weintraub, J. K. (1989). Assessing coping strategies: A theoretically based approach. *Journal of Personality and Social Psychology, 56*(2), 267–283. https://doi.org/10.1037/0022-3514.56.2.267.

Ernest, P., Hopkins, J., Emke, M., Germain-Rutherford, A., Heiser, S., Robbins, J., & Stickler, U. (2019). New media in language education. In D. Newby, M. Cavalli, & F. Heyworth (Eds.) *Changing contexts, evolving competences: 25 years of inspiring innovation in language education* (pp. 89–99). Council of Europe Publishing,.

Hodges, C., Moore, S., Lockee, B., Trust, T., & Bond, A. (2020). The difference between emergency remote teaching and online learning. *Educause Review,* (March 27, 2020). https://er.educause.edu/articles/2020/3/the-difference-between-emergency-remote-teaching-and-online-learning.

Karppinen, P. (2005). Meaningful learning with digital and online videos: Theoretical perspectives. *Association for the Advancement of Computing in Education, 13*(3), 233–250. http://www.aace.org/pubs/aacej

Littlejohn, A. (2020). Seeking and sending signals: Remodelling teaching practice during the Covid-19 crisis. *Contemporary Issues in Education, 40*(1), 56–62. https://doi.org/10.46786/ac20.8253

Llanes, M. (2019). Digital teaching competences of pre-service teachers. In D. Masats, M. Mont, & N. González-Acevedo (Eds.) *Joint efforts for innovation* (pp. 47–52). Paragon Publishing. https://doi.org/10.5281/zenodo.3064130

MacIntyre, P. D., Gregersen, T., & Mercer, S. (2020). Language teachers' coping strategies during the Covid-19 conversion to online teaching: Correlations with stress, wellbeing and negative emotions. *System*, *94*, 1–13. http.://doi.org/10.1016/j.system.2020.102352

Meskill, C., & Sadykova, G. (2011). Introducing EFL faculty to online instructional conversations. *ReCALL*, *23*(3), 200–217. https://doi.org/10.1017/S0958344011000140

Moser, K.M., Wei, T., & Brenner, D. (2020). Remote teaching during Covid-19: Implications from a national survey of language educators. *System*, *97*, 1–15. https://doi.org/10.1016/j.system.2020.102431

Robbins, J. (2020). *Language learner engagement in asynchronous discussion forums: an exploratory study.* [Doctoral dissertation]. Universitat Autònoma de Barcelona, Spain. http://hdl.handle.net/10803/671302

Schleicher, A. (2020). Education disrupted - Education rebuilt. Spotlight: Quality education for all during Covid-19 crisis. *OECD/Hundred Research Report #011.* https://hundred-cdn.s3.amazonaws.com/uploads/report/file/15/hundred_spotlight_Covid-19_digital.pdf

Stanojević, M. M. (2015). Developing online teaching skills: The DOTS project. In R. Hampel, & U. Stickler (Eds.), *Developing online language teaching: Research-based pedagogies and reflective practices* (pp. 150-162). Palgrave Macmillan.

Stickler, U., Hampel, R., & Emke, M. (2020). A developmental framework for online language teaching skills. *Australian Journal of Applied Linguistics*, *3*(1), 133–151. https://doi.org/10.29140/ajal.v3n1.271

Tran, A., Burns, A., & Ollerhead, S. (2017). ELT lecturers' experiences of a new research policy: Exploring emotion and academic identity. *System*, *67*, 65–76. https://doi.org/10.1016/j.system.2017.04.014

5
"Moving your language teaching online" Toolkit: Teachers' early reflections on their experience and skills

Karina von Lindeiner-Stráský
Hélène Pulker
Elodie Vialleton

Introduction

As the Covid-19 virus spread in spring 2020, educational institutions of all levels were forced to shut their doors, and conventional ways of teaching and learning were interrupted across the world for months or years (UNESCO, 2021). The need to uphold access to education led to a sudden move to online teaching. This new experience was challenging for many practitioners with no or little practice in online teaching, and particularly daunting and stressful for language teachers whose practice usually involves emphasis on interactivity and communication between teachers and learners, often perceived as more difficult online.

Internationally, language teachers sought support from the UK Open University (OU), where distance and online language teaching is long-established. In response, experienced online language teachers and researchers at the OU rapidly developed the *Moving your language teaching online* Toolkit to assist Higher Education language teachers during the crisis. It was produced and shared as a free open digital resource (OpenLearn Create, 2020), and free workshops were organised online to share expertise and ideas, reflect on experiences, and discuss good practice. The Toolkit was accessed and downloaded thousands of times, and nearly 200 teachers attended the free workshops in late 2020, confirming that the initiative met considerable demand.

This presented a unique opportunity for researchers to investigate the experience of a large cohort of practitioners moving to online teaching at scale and at pace. This chapter examines this through the analysis of the reflections of teachers collected during a 'Moving your language teaching online' workshop. With reference to the key principles of online language teaching which underpin the design of the Toolkit, and to Hampel and Stickler's skills pyramid framework (2005), we examine how teachers perceived their proficiency in terms of online language teaching skills after the move to online teaching, how they experienced this move, and how they perceived their role as online language teachers during the crisis.

Key principles of online language teaching

Online language teaching is a long-established field, branching out from the wider and earlier field of computer-assisted language learning (CALL) that has existed for over three decades and predates the emergence of online technology. Both fields also build on principles of distance education, developed well before computers became mainstream. This section outlines the principles of online and distance language teaching which underpinned the design of the *Moving your language teaching online* Toolkit and structured the workshop discussions which form our research data.

Despite decades of successful implementation, CALL and online learning and teaching scholars sometimes feel that they have to defend their research or its definition (Levy & Hubbard, 2005) to colleagues in language studies and the humanities (Gillepsie, 2020). But due to the pandemic, language teachers now need knowledge of online learning and teaching principles to adapt to their new teaching environments.

Early work on teacher training and CALL focuses on establishing whether specific online pedagogy is needed when being assisted by a computer to teach languages. Colpaert (2006) suggests that there is no online pedagogy, arguing that teaching online forces us to reconsider our assumptions about language teaching, but that technology should not shape teaching methods. We agree with Colpaert, but in our experience technologies make new and different cognitive demands on teachers (Hampel & Stickler, 2005; Stickler & Hauck, 2006; Comas-Quinn, 2011). Even though language teaching pedagogy overall heavily relies on communicative and task-based approaches, teaching languages online requires factoring-in new elements. These can be grouped into the four key principles outlined below.

Defining online learning spaces

Language teaching today is mainly based on socio-cultural theories of learning informed by pedagogical principles such as interaction, collaboration, learner control and community (Beaven *et al.*, 2010). The online environment provides opportunities for a more learner-centred approach and increased interaction among students and between students and teachers, for socialising, communicating, and collaborating. Students can work with peers and teachers but also with the wider world, accessing authentic online materials and communities or participating in virtual exchanges. The teacher's role in facilitating this is crucial. Teachers need to be aware that online environments provide potentially different spatial and temporal characteristics and different rules of engagement compared to face-to-face classrooms. Learning spaces (such as learning management systems, forums, and online rooms) need to be defined in order to avoid misunderstandings, confusion, or unacceptable behaviour (Stickler & Hampel, 2015).

Developing a teaching presence

Online environments change the nature of interactions between teacher, student, and content, requiring a re-examination of teachers' roles in enhancing students' learning (Baran, 2011). As online students are expected to take greater control of their learning and actively stimulate their peers' learning, facilitation emerges as an important teacher role (Vetter, 2004; Comas-Quinn, 2011). While still focussing on their responsibilities as teachers in online courses, teachers move from being at the centre of the interaction and information to being "animateur[s]" (Vetter, 2004), whilst the approach strongly shifts from instruction to knowledge construction (Stickler & Hauck, 2006). Teachers need to create a new identity for themselves in this environment, having to develop an online teaching presence that consists of designing and organising learning opportunities, providing timely information and direction, facilitating interaction, collaboration, and reflection, and offering support to learners, ensuring that the community of learners reaches the intended learning outcomes while responding to individual learners' needs. The teaching presence in online learning is a significant influential factor for student satisfaction (Garrison, Cleveland-Innes, & Fung, 2010).

Integrating technology and pedagogy

Online environments are dynamic and multimodal. Technology-focused programmes, which consider that separate skills have to be required for different tools, have evolved into integrated approaches encouraging teachers to engage in pedagogical problem-solving and exploration of online teaching and materials (Stickler & Hampel, 2015). Exploring the new affordances of online tools for synchronous and asynchronous communications, while understanding their constraints, can inspire language teachers to design innovative approaches to teach and assess skills and knowledge. Through exploration of the functionalities of the online environment (e.g. multimodality), teachers can reflect on different approaches to online language pedagogies and take advantage of the affordances of online tools to add value compared to offline learning approaches, e.g. by using forums to foster interaction, wikis for collaborative tasks, or student-managed online rooms for speaking practice.

Supporting students' needs

Murphy, Shelley, and Baumann (2010) show that learners reported anxiety in online chat rooms and a greater need for directions, motivation and self-regulation. They concluded that distance language teaching is essentially a learner support role, strongly underpinned by affective and organisational dimensions of tutor practice (p. 132). Murphy *et al.*, (2011) found that distance and online language learners value approachable, supportive, committed, enthusiastic and encouraging teachers especially in online and distance context, where contact might be less frequent and maintaining motivation can be problematic. Equally important is the ability to empathise with students, to understand individual concerns or difficulties with the course.

The above demonstrates that distance and online teaching relies on defined pedagogic principles. Hampel and Stickler (2005) showed it also requires specific and complex skills on the part of teachers, proposing a systematic framework, the skills pyramid, to describe them. Compton (2009) also proposed a framework, which separates rather than integrates technology and pedagogy. Hampel and Stickler revisited their findings ten years after their initial research, to take into account new developments, finding that teachers' online language teaching skills evolved as technology became more widespread. They therefore adjusted their framework in Stickler and Hampel (2015), with significant implications for theory and practice. The move to online teaching at the start of the Covid-19 pandemic provided a new opportunity to examine how teachers' online language teaching skills have evolved since.

Toolkit design

The *Moving your language teaching online* Toolkit supports university language teachers in understanding the key principles and developing the skills outlined above. It gives practical advice based on a coherent and pedagogically-informed framework for online language teaching. Associated Toolkit workshops and an asynchronous forum provided spaces for practitioners to exchange knowledge and share good practice as a community.

The Toolkit consists of nine help sheets, reflecting the OU's previously released help sheets on distance teaching (Institute of Technology, 2020). They each cover one aspect of online language teaching, underpinned by the key principles of online language teaching defined in Table 5.1.

The help sheets provide overviews, examples of teaching practices, and advice. For example, "Creating an online classroom" provides introductory ideas using two different scenarios (using a full online platform as a hub for a course or using just a single tool like a forum as a starting point). It discusses practicalities, advantages and disadvantages of adapting face-to-face classrooms in an online scenario, guiding teachers to list the typical components of their own language teaching (e.g., lesson starters, discussions, lectures, activities developing language skills, etc.), examining ideas to transfer these to an online or blended learning environ-

Table 5.1 *Content and underpinning principles of the Moving your language teach-*

Number	Title	Main Underpinning Principle
Help sheet 1	Creating an online classroom	Defining online learning spaces
Help sheet 2	Creating an online community	Developing a teaching presence
Help sheet 3	Developing your teaching voice online	Developing a teaching presence
Help sheet 4	Teaching language skills online	Integrating technology and pedagogy
Help sheet 5	Facilitating a language tutorial online	Integrating technology and pedagogy
Help sheet 6	Maintaining motivation	Supporting students' needs
Help sheet 7	Developing assessment strategies	Integrating technology and pedagogy
Help sheet 8	Using a learning management system	Defining online learning spaces
Help sheet 9	Reflecting on the blend that's best for your own learners	All

ment. The final section encourages reflection on and adapting to their individual teaching situation by listing further questions to identify relevant issues.

The Toolkit is not intended as a one-size-fits-all key to successful online language teaching, but as a point of reference for online language teaching and thus as support and inspiration to teachers designing their distance classes according to their and their students' needs.

Two online workshops accompanied the Toolkit publication, providing an opportunity for participants to discuss the principles of online language teaching that underpin the Toolkit design, and to reflect on their own experience and skills. The research presented in this chapter focusses on the reflections of teachers following the transition to online teaching collected at the first of these workshops.

Research methodology

Research questions

The aim of our research was to explore, through discussions about the Toolkit, the experience and skills of teachers following the move to online teaching triggered by the Covid-19 pandemic. Three research questions guided the workshop discussions:

1. What was the participants' perception of their level of proficiency in terms of online language teaching skills?

2. How did university language teachers experience the move to online teaching in the context of the Covid-19 pandemic?

3. How did participants perceive their role as online language teachers in the context of the Covid-19 pandemic?

Table 5.2 *Summary workshop information*

Launch Event Dates	30 October and 13 November, 2020
Number of registrations	400
Number of attendees	Over 200 (exact number unavailable)
Number of participants in the text chats	185
Number of contributions posted	856

Data collection

Data was collected during two workshops (see Table 5.2) with a self-selected group of higher education language teaching practitioners. Attendees from 36 UK universities and seven universities in four EU countries represented twelve different languages taught. 72% had not taught languages online before the start of Covid-19, and 28% had received no specific training on online language teaching. 66% were teaching online only at the time of the workshop, 28% were delivering a blend of online and face-to-face teaching.

Much of the interaction between participants and between facilitators and participants took place in writing, through a synchronous chat discussion involving 185 participants who posted a total of 856 contributions. The text chat follows the sequence of the workshops' spoken discussions and reveals the questions and reflections of the participants based on their experiences. This data can be described as brief textual contributions, sometimes fragmented, part of a fast-paced, highly interactive informal exchange. Their concise and fragmented nature means that the depth of arguments is limited, but because they involve many more participants than the spoken contributions, they better represent the diverse experiences and views of the participants.

Data analysis

This chapter is based on the data collected at the first of the two workshops. The content of the text chat, fully anonymised, was coded using qualitative data analysis software. We analysed the data iteratively, taking both a deductive and inductive approach. Firstly, we used the online language tutors skills pyramid levels developed by Hampel and Stickler (2005), later adapted in Stickler and Hampel (2015), as a framework for coding. The 2005 model was used primarily as it allowed for more fine-grained coding whilst still enabling us to match the analysis and findings to the 2015 model. This led to a quantitative (Neuendorf, 2017) and qualitative (Dörnyei, 2007) content analysis based on the framework. For this dual analysis, the content of the text chat contributions was matched to the levels of Hampel and Stickler's 2005 skills pyramid. Codes were checked for accuracy and consistency, and adjustments were made before analysis. However, our coding and analysis must be understood as forming part of an interpretative qualitative research approach, and we acknowledge the subjectivity of the coding and understand the limitations of the consistency we make claims for.

Figure 5.1 provides definitions and explanations of the levels based on Hampel and Stickler (2005, pp. 319-320) and Stickler and Hampel (2015, p. 66), and examples of content from our corpus coded at those levels.

We then coded the data inductively, using the thematic analysis methodology (Braun & Clarke, 2006), to identify other common themes emerging from the data, as described in our findings.

Findings

Table 5.3 presents a quantitative view of the deductive coding of our data based on the seven levels of Hampel and Stickler's skills pyramid framework (2005), reflecting the most frequently discussed skills during the workshops.

The highest volume of discussion relates to level 3 of the 2005 skills pyramid: "dealing with the constraints and possibilities of the medium." The second most frequent level was level 4: "online socialisation," followed by level 5: "facilitating communicative competence" and level 6: "creativity and choice." Based on our coding, no contribution aligned to levels 1, 2 or 7: "basic ICT competence," "specific technical competence for the software," and "own style." The findings from our thematic analysis presented below are therefore related to levels 3, 4, 5, and 6 of the skills pyramid.

Level 3: Dealing with constraints and possibilities of the medium

Two main strands could be identified for this level: contributions centred on technology only, and contributions on the best use of technology for pedagogic purpose.

The first strand mainly consisted in exchanges and recommendations about technology and online tools, especially tools enabling collaboration and gamification in language teaching and learning. Challenges related to using too many different resources were mentioned; for example, one participant wrote:

> *'when we use too many different tools students can get confused'.*

The second strand comprised of contributions relating the use of technology to pedagogy. It included five different types of threads:

- threads on the use and mix of asynchronous vs synchronous online tools to accommodate speaking practice, to operate 'flipped classrooms', or reflecting on how to make best use of synchronous sessions and on what students can do independently and asynchronously, for example:

	LEVELS IN THE 2015 FRAMEWORK	LEVELS IN THE 2005 FRAMEWORK	DEFINITIONS FROM THE AUTHORS (2005)	EXAMPLES FROM OUR DATA
higher competence ↑	Creativity, choice and own style	Own style	Developing one's own personal teaching style, using the materials and media to their best advantage, forming a rapport with students, and using resources creatively to promote active and communicative language learning	none
		Creativity and choice	Creating or selecting online activities with the communicative principles in mind	'I have found useful creating activities that involve collaborative learning, such as peer review podcast, recorded discussions'
	Facilitating communicative competence and online socialization	Facilitating communicative competence	Facilitating communicative competence	'In asynchronous teaching I put as much voice as possible and in synchronous sessions I am as silent as possible and mostly write in the chat and take notes'
		Online socialization	Creating a sense of community in the classroom	'I encourage [students] to join live sessions 15 minutes earlier to chat among each other' 'encouraging emoji use/interactivity is key. And also not interpreting silence as lack of interest or engagement'
	Specific technical competence and dealing with constraints and possibilities of the medium	Dealing with constraints and possibilities of the medium	Dealing with constraints and affordances of the particular software used	'I use breakout rooms for small group work' 'challenge: students are reluctant to put their webcam on'
		Specific technical competence for the software	Using the specific software applications needed to teach	none
↓ lower competence	Basic ICT competence	Basic ICT competence	Using networked computers and familiarity with common commands and applications	none

Figure 5.1 *Online teaching skill levels, adapted from the pyramid from Hampel and Stickler (2005) and Stickler and Hampel (2015)*

"We use discussion boards, Padlet (asynchronously) as part of the course, and [...] some students have also organised themselves to chat outside the class (Facebook, Whatsapp). Use of breakout rooms for speaking tasks during the live class (synchronously)."

This links to themes of student independence and student-generated resources (see next section):
- threads on the use of breakout rooms and the affordances of various

Table 5.3 *Frequency of levels coded*

Pyramid levels (2005)	Percentage of chat contributions coded at levels
Basic ICT competence	0
Specific technical competence for the software	0
Dealing with the constraints and possibilities of the medium	61%
Online socialization	26%
Facilitating communicative competence	8%
Creativity and choice	5%
Own style	0%

tools to organise classes and groups, for example:

"Start with very easy tasks in breakouts so that they get to know each other and gain confidence."

- comments on challenges specific to some languages, in particular in relation to developing writing skills in languages with scripts different from English, e.g. in Arabic:

"I find the whiteboard excellent in teaching writing in Arabic."

- mentions of and questions about affordances and constraints of technology for assessment, such as invigilating software, for example:

"Do any of you use proctoring software? What is your experience?"

- threads on the use of microphones and webcams, including comments about muting microphones to boost student confidence, about dealing with shy students and how and when to encourage students to unmute mics and turn on cameras, for example:

"Practising language with the mic off is an advantage to online tutorials and quite freeing for students!"

There were multiple contributions about the role of cameras and of non-verbal communication and the use of text chat, emojis and games to encourage communication.

Level 4: Online socialisation

On this level, there were contributions on the use of tools (e.g. discussion boards, online polls) and strategies (e.g. group sizes, mix of synchronous and asynchronous activities, use of breakout rooms) to develop a sense of community and facilitate online socialisation and interaction for students. Participants reported organising social events or slots as part of their classes to create and foster a sense of community or break isolation, as described in the following example:

> *"Many students are probably feeling quite isolated right now, so I reckon building in more interaction is really important both from a pedagogical and more holistic perspective."*

Others linked the social dimension of language learning and the need to develop the confidence of students to interact in the target language, but this angle was not frequently developed, and most of the contributions were about basic socialisation and pastoral concerns for students. Some linked to the theme of students' and teachers' wellbeing, as described in the next section.

Level 5: Facilitating communicative competence

Regarding facilitating communicative competence, participants mentioned ideas such as ring-fencing time in synchronous sessions for the development of speaking skills, or the creation of conversation clubs. There was considerable interest in the difference between speaking production and speaking interaction, and how to approach them. Interestingly, some teachers welcomed a renewed focus on pronunciation and speaking production *per se*, potentially veering away from a communicative approach. For example:

> *"I love the way speaking on vocal forums places an emphasis back on spoken production independently from interaction."*

Others linked communicative competence to the development of cultural knowledge and discussed using online visual prompts to support this. The relatively low quantity of data related to level 5 will be addressed in the discussion section.

Level 6: Creativity and choice

Some teachers were evidently highly skilful in online language teaching and had smoothly transitioned to online teaching. Our data shows that some teachers implemented complex teaching strategies, such as combining the use of different tools, considering the respective roles of synchronous and asynchronous activities, or showing creative pedagogic approaches making use of the affordances of online tools. One participant commented:

> *"About the webcam topic: previous small games work well! Ask simple questions such as 'are you drinking a coffee?" yes = turn on camera / no = turn off camera. Afterwards they are not so shy!"*

Similarly high levels of skills were also reflected in text chat contributions related to the changes required to assess students remotely. Some teachers expressed that they had learned new skills or deployed new strategies which they would continue to use after the return to classroom-based teaching:

> *"The forced move to online can help perhaps bring about long term change."*
>
> *"I have heard so many other colleagues say this <name>, it's given them a push to do things differently and they really like it!"*

Two specific examples of new practices that emerged from the transition to online teaching shared by two participants were "making much more use of audio recordings" and "[doing] continuous assessment."

Other levels and findings

We did not code any of our data against levels 1, 2, or 7. The inductive coding of the data enabled us to identify different common themes emerging from the teachers' text chat contributions. Both matters will be discussed in the next section.

Discussion

Referring back to our research questions, we now report on what the findings of our analysis reveal about the experience of teachers who moved their language teaching online during the Covid-19 pandemic, and on their perceived skills and role as online language teachers. We consider how this aligns with the skills pyramid conceptualised by Hampel and Stickler (2005) and Stickler and Hampel (2015), and how it compares with the experience of earlier adopters of online language teaching as documented in the literature.

Research question 1: What was the participants' perception of their level of proficiency in terms of online language teaching skills?

First, we found that **skills related to the use of technology can be taken for granted.** There was no match to levels 1 and 2 of the 2005 pyramid in our data, indicating that participants did not seem to have been concerned with the use of technology *per se*. This suggests that the basic use of technology, including generic and specific hardware and software, was unproblematic. This was confirmed by findings presented above, for example, the fact that training needs reported by participants related to higher levels of the skills pyramid: teachers demonstrated concerns with integrating pedagogy and technology rather than with software-specific training. This probably reflects the generalised used of technology as part of face-to-face and blended language teaching today, which may be considered as normalised (Bax, 2003, 2011).

Second, we found that **teachers focused strongly on making use of the affordances of the online medium.** Many of the participants' contributions could be matched to level 3 of the 2005 pyramid, "dealing with the constraints and possibilities of the medium," suggesting that this level of competence was not taken for granted by all of our participants. Most of the questioning related to linking the use of technology to sound pedagogic principles. This is consistent with findings from our thematic analysis showing that many text chat contributions focussed on comparing face-to-face with online pedagogies.

Third, **teachers prioritised creating a sense of community, but not explicitly to facilitate L2 communicative competence.** According to our data, creating a sense of community in the classroom was one of the teachers' strongest preoccupations concerning online teaching. The significant amount of data related to level 4 of the 2005 pyramid suggests, amongst our participants, a will to address the challenge of fostering exchanges online, and of developing a sense of community for groups of students who were dispersed during the pandemic, consistent with the high interest in the Toolkit help sheets on "creating an online community" and "developing your teaching voice online."

The difference between levels 4 ("online socialisation") and 5 ("facilitating communicative competence") in our data coding lies in whether socialisation and communication were addressed generically (level 4) or in relation to the development of target language skills (level 5) within a communicative approach to language teaching (Widdowson, 1978; Canale & Swain, 1980). The relatively low volume of data coded at level 5 raises questions about how successfully teachers were able to transfer their specialist language teaching approach and pedagogy to an online setting. Such questions are confirmed by the very high interest shown in the Toolkit help sheet on "teaching language skills online." They are also linked to inductive thematic findings revealing frequent questioning about how to develop speaking and interaction skills online. This suggests a need for subject-specific training for online teaching (Hampel and Stickler, 2005). We acknowledge that the low volume of coded data related to "facilitating communicative competence" could be attributed to the fact that teachers do not always explicitly articulate their pedagogic approaches in training sessions (Ur, 2019).

Our findings related to "creativity" and "own style" of teaching are addressed in the next sub-sections.

Research question 2: How did university language teachers experience the move to online teaching in the context of the Covid-19 pandemic?

We found that most teachers were enthusiastic about online teaching, and some displayed creative student-focused approaches. Our inductive data analysis shows that attitudes towards online teaching were predominantly positive. This is consistent with the information collected during the workshop as part of an interactive poll activity through which 59% of participants agreed or strongly agreed that they enjoyed teaching online, despite mostly feeling "challenged" about it. Many participants had integrated some CALL tools and principles of online language teaching described in Section 2 to their face-to-face teaching prior to the move to online teaching. It is likely that the particularly long history of computer-aided learning within the languages field contributed to the positive outlook of the majority of our participants when they pivoted online.

Some contributions captured in our data evidence that teachers were able to create or select online resources and activities which support the communicative principles underpinning language learning and teaching, matching level 6 of the 2005 skills pyramid, "creativity and choice." For example, some discussed the balance and purpose of synchronous and asynchronous teaching. Their reflections suggest that with time, facilitation of communicative competence could be enhanced as they become more confident at creating and selecting activities creatively, with this aim in mind.

Research question 3: How did participants perceive their role as online language teachers in the context of the Covid-19 pandemic?

Emerging own styles

We did not code any of our data against level 7, "***own style***," defined as "personal teaching style, using the materials and media to their best advantage, forming a rapport with […] students and using the resources creatively to promote active and communicative language learning" (Hampel & Stickler, 2005, p. 319). Caution is needed before interpreting this. Evidencing the development of a personal teaching style requires time and deeper exchanges than text chat contributions allowed. The absence of references to level 7 could be explained by the fragmented nature of brief text chat contributions which are less likely to reflect the complexity of personal, creative approaches and skills. It is also possible that there was a low number of teachers with sufficient prior experience of online language teaching to have developed skills at the highest level only a few months after the move to online teaching and learning due to Covid-19, or that highly skilled teachers may not have signed up for our workshops.

However, our inductive thematic analysis indicates that participants saw their own role online evolve from teachers to facilitators whose main focus was student-centred. It also suggests that teachers focussed strongly on forming a rapport with students, **supporting their wellbeing**, and developing more **student-centred pedagogies**, revealing emerging aspects of their "own style."

The role of online teachers, from the early days of online language teaching to the Covid-19 pandemic

Our analysis reveals similar conclusions concerning the challenges faced by online language teachers compared to those we encountered when we introduced online language courses at the Open University in the early 2000s. It also reflects what the literature has documented: teachers are concerned with integrating technology and pedagogy (Ertmer, 2005; Colpaert, 2006; Stickler & Hauck, 2006), recognising the importance of considering affordances and constraints of online tools and design activities carefully (Hampel, 2009). They see it as their role to help students navigate the increased complexity of their learning environment (Hampel & Stickler, 2005), acknowledging that teaching language skills online effectively presents challenges (Beaven *et al.*, 2010), and understanding that their role has to change as they become facilitators of learning (Stickler & Hauck, 2006; Comas-Quinn, 2011) while their classes become more student-centred and their role takes a pastoral dimension (Hauck & Hampel, 2005). Some of our participants took this further, trialling the use of student-generated content as part of encouraging students to play a more active part in their learning. This suggests that "***teaching with students***" is perhaps a new dimension of the portfolio of skills evidenced by highly proficient online language teachers.

Implications for theory and practice

The first change in Stickler and Hampel's revised model (2015) was to focus "more on the levels beyond the basic ICT competence which today tends to be taken for granted" (p. 65). Their adapted skills pyramid (p. 66) therefore labels "basic ICT competence" as level 0. Our data suggests that this evolution has continued: for our participants, "specific technical competence" can also be taken for granted and integrated alongside "basic ICT competence."

In our data, "dealing with the constraints and possibilities of the medium," however, is a step up from competence in using basic and specific technology and cannot fully be taken for granted. Furthermore, for our participants, "facilitating communicative competence" requires a higher level of experience and skills in online language teaching compared to "online socialisation." This differs from Stickler and Hampel's adapted pyramid (2015) which merged the two levels. However, our participants' perceived role related to socialisation involved the additional aspect of supporting their students' wellbeing. Finally, the 2015 skills pyramid merges levels 6 and 7 of the 2005 model into a single level 3 labelled "creativity, choice, and own style." Our data does not bring evidence that this might have changed but suggests that "teaching with students" is perhaps an additional dimension evidenced by the most proficient of online language teachers.

Figure 5.2 summarises how our findings align with the 2005 and 2015 versions of the skills pyramid, reflecting how our participants' competence with online teaching skills in the early stages of the Covid-19 pandemic compares with previous research findings.

In terms of practice, our data demonstrates that participants welcomed the workshops as an opportunity to share and reflect on their experience. They felt reassured to see that they faced the same challenges and expressed a need to discuss pedagogy and an interest in sharing good practice with each other. This will guide us in further developing the Toolkit initiative to continue supporting colleagues. Further research can ascertain whether the initiative was effective in creating a community of practice and whether it successfully improved online language teaching practice in Higher Education.

Conclusion and future plans

The Toolkit was designed primarily as a practical tool to support teachers in a time of crisis. The high attendance and lively discussion at the launch workshops, including the numerous text chat interactions, as well as the Toolkit's high download numbers suggest that it addressed a need for language teachers in the Covid-19 pandemic. In the future, it remains available as a free resource create for teacher training on OpenLearn Create (Open University, 2022). Thus, it is likely to extend its relevance beyond the immediate crisis as there are already strong indications that many teachers will retain elements of online teaching as part of their regular practice.

Our research provided valuable data to examine the actual online language teaching practices of a diverse group of teachers, albeit on the basis of a self-selecting group, and to compare this to the research findings of the past three decades. While it remains to be seen whether online teaching will remain mainstream, a move towards a wider and more general application of online language teaching principles might allow for verification and further investigation of our findings.

The workshops provided an insight into participants' perception of their role as online language teachers in the difficult conditions of the pandemic, which in the future could be used as a starting point for investigating the experiences and perceptions of language teachers in an increasingly digitalised learning environment. In the future, we plan to collect further data and provide more analysis to explore teachers' practices in online language teaching post pandemic. This could be examined together with the questions of whether and how the Toolkit may have supported the professional development of language teachers and/or provided strategies for online language teaching. Further research would thus contribute to the integration of training and evaluation, teaching and research, and theory and practice.

Acknowledgements

We acknowledge the contribution of the participants who shared their perspectives through the "Moving your language teaching online" work-

	Levels in the 2005 framework	Levels in the 2015 framework	Our data
Higher competence ↑	7. Own Style	3. Creativity, choice and own style	4. Creativity, choice and own style; teaching with students
	6. Creativity and choice		
	5. Facilitating communicative competence	2. Facilitating communicative competence and online socialisation	3. Facilitating communicative competence
	4. Online socialisation		2. Online socialisation and student wellbeing
	3. Dealing with constraints and possibilities of the medium	1. Specific technical competence and dealing with constraints and possibilities of the medium	1. Dealing with constraints and possibilities of the medium
	2. Specific technical competence for the software		
Lower competence ↓	1. Basic ICT competence		
Taken for granted		0. Basic ICT competence	0. Basic ICT competence and specific technical competence for the software

Figure 5.2 *Aligning our data to the skills pyramid frameworks of Hampel and Stickler (2005) and Stickler and Hampel (2015)*

shops and our colleagues on the Toolkit team: Zsuzsanna Barkanyi, Christine Pleines, Anna Calvi, and Kim Richmond.

References

Baran, E., Correira, A-P. & Thompson, A. (2021). Transforming online teaching practice: critical analysis of the literature on the roles and competencies of online teachers, *Distance Education, 32*(3), 421–439. https://doi.org/10.1080/01587919.2011.610293.

Bax, S. (2003). CALL - past, present, and future. *System, 31*(1), 13–28. https://doi.org/10.1016/S0346- 251X(02)00071-4.

Bax, S. (2011). Normalisation Revisited: The Effective Use of Technology in Language Education. *International Journal of Computer-Assisted Language Learning and Teaching (IJCALLT), 1*(2), 1-15. https://doi.org/10.4018/ijcallt.2011040101

Beaven, T., Emke, M., Ernest, P., Germain-Rutherford, A., Hampel, R., Hopkins, J., Stanojevic, M. & Stickler, U. (2010). Needs and challenges for online language teachers - the ECML project DOTS. *Teaching English with Technology: A Journal for Teachers of English, 10*(2), 5–20.

Braun, V., & Clarke, V. (2006) Using thematic analysis in psychology. *Qualitative Research in Psychology, 3*(2), 77–101. https://doi.org/10.1191/1478088706QP063OA.

Canale, M. & Swain, M. (1980). Theoretical bases of communicative approaches to second language teaching and testing. *Applied Linguistics, 1*

(1), 1–47. https://doi.org/10.1093/applin/I.1.1

Colpaert, J. (2006). Pedagogy-driven design for online language teaching and learning. *CALICO Journal, 23*(3), 447–497.

Comas-Quinn, A. (2011). Learning to teach online or learning to become an online teacher: an exploration of teachers' experiences in a blended learning course. *ReCALL,* 23(3) 218–232.

Compton, L. (2009). Preparing language teachers to teach language online: a look at skills, roles, and responsibilities. *Computer Assisted Language Learning, 22*(1), 73–99. https://doi.org/10.1080/09588220802613831

Dörnyei, Z. (2007) *Research methods in applied linguistics.* Oxford University Press.

Ertmer, P. (2005). Teacher pedagogical beliefs: The final frontier in our quest for technology integration. *Educational Technology Research and Development, 53*(4), 25–39.

Garrison, D., Cleveland-Innes, M. & Fung, T. (2010). Exploring causal relationships among teaching, cognitive and social presence: Student perception of the community of inquiry framework. *The Internet and Higher Education, 13*(1–2), 31–36. https://doi.org/10.1016/j.iheduc.2009.10.002

Gillepsie, J. (2020). CALL research: Where are we now? *ReCALL, 32*(2), 127–144. https://doi.org/10.1017/S0958344020000051.

Hampel, R. (2009). Training teachers for the multimedia age: Developing teacher expertise to enhance online learner interaction and collaboration. *Innovation in Language Learning and Teaching, 3*(1), 35–50.

Hampel, R. & Stickler, U. (2005). New skills for new classrooms: Training tutors to teach languages online. *Computer Assisted Language Learning, 18*(4), 311–326. https://doi.org/10.1080/09588220500335455.

Hauck, M. & Hampel, R. (2005). The challenge of implementing online tuition in distance language courses: Task design and tutor role. In B. Holmberg, M. Shelley, & C. White (Eds.), *Distance education and languages: Evolution and change* (pp. 258–277). Multilingual Matters.

Institute of Educational Technology (2020). *Teaching at a distance: Helpsheet series.* https://iet.open.ac.uk/teaching-at-a-distance

Levy, M. & Hubbard, P. (2005). Why call CALL "CALL"? *Computer Assisted Language Learning, 18*(3), 143–149. https://doi.org/10.1080/09588220500208884.

Murphy, L., Shelley, M. & Baumann, U. (2010). Qualities of effective tutors in distance language teaching: student perceptions. *Innovation in Language Learning and Teaching, 4*(2), 119–136. https://doi.org/10.1080/17501220903414342.

Murphy, L., Shelley, M., White, C., & Baumann, U. (2011). Tutor and student perceptions of what makes an effective distance language teacher. *Distance Education, 32*(3), 397–419. https://doi.org/10.1080/015879192011610290.

Neuendorf, K. A. (2017). *The content analysis guidebook* (2nd ed.). SAGE Publications. https://doi.org/10.4135/9781071802878.
OpenLearn Create (2020). *Moving your language teaching online – a Toolkit.* https://www.open.edu/openlearncreate/course/view.php?id=6341
Stickler, U. & Hampel, R. (2015). Transforming teaching: New skills for online language learning spaces. In R. Hampel & U. Stickler (Eds.), *Developing online language teaching: Research-based pedagogies and reflective practices.* (pp. 63–77). Palgrave Macmillan.
Stickler, U., Hampel, R., & Emke, M. (2020). A developmental framework for online language teaching skills. *Australian Journal of Applied Linguistics, 3*(1), 133–151. https://doi.org/10.29140/ajal.v3n1.271
Stickler, U., & Hauck, M. (2006). What does it take to teach online? Toward a pedagogy for online language teaching and learning. *CALICO Journal, 23*(3), 463–734. https://doi.org/10.1558/cj.v23i3.463-475
UNESCO (2021). *Education: From disruption to recovery.* https://en.unesco.org/Covid19/educationresponse
Ur, P. (2019). Theory and practice in language teacher education, *Language Teaching 52*(1), 450-459. https://doi.org/10.1017/S0261444819000090.
Vetter, A. (2004). Les spécificités du tutorat à distance à l'Open University: enseigner les langues avec Lyceum. *Apprentissage des Langues et Systèmes d'Information et Communication, 7*, 107–129. https://doi.org/10.4000/alsic.2310
Widdowson, H. (1978). *Teaching language as communication.* Oxford University Press.

6
Transitioning to online teaching: Language teacher wellbeing during the Covid-19 crisis

Sun Shin

Amongst the many challenges which affect teaching under normal circumstances, transitioning to online/remote formats during the Covid-19 crisis increased the levels of stress for teachers (MacIntyre, Gregersen, & Mercer, 2020). Many teachers have been forced to adapt to a whole new world of teaching—following new regulations and guiding their students into learning remotely while also tackling stressors in their private lives (Kim & Asbury, 2020).

While many teachers have been adapting and coming up with their own strategies for coping, others have been struggling and suffering from deteriorating physical and mental health (Aperribai *et al.*, 2020). This chapter aims to offer a deeper insight into the experiences of four language teachers at Korean universities during the sudden change to online teaching, the stressors they faced, and how they coped with these challenges. Understanding the wellbeing of teachers and the coping strategies they utilised has important implications not only during this crisis but also beyond for future teachers facing any form of a professional period of disruption.

Background to the study

Language teacher stressors and wellbeing

Previous research has identified various sources of stress for teachers, such as heavy workload, discipline issues, role conflict, bureaucracy, lack of effective communication, and demanding interpersonal work (Day & Gu, 2009; Johnson *et al.*, 2005). For language teachers specifically, additional stressors have been identified, including unstable job contracts (Mercer, 2020), language anxiety (Horwitz, 1996), and cultural challenges of working abroad (Luk, 2012); thus, language teachers are prone to higher risks of burnout (MacIntyre *et al.*, 2020). In addition, increased demands of information and communication technologies in language learning require language teachers to be multiskilled not only in pedagogy and didactics but in using a range of digital tools as well (Stickler, Hampel, & Emke, 2020). Naturally, this has become especially pertinent for those who have switched to online teaching during the Covid-19 outbreak.

Wellbeing has been typically described from a hedonic or eudemonic perspective (Ryan & Deci, 2001). A hedonic perspective focuses on the experience of pleasure and satisfaction and, thus, is subjectively determined by positive mental states (Kahneman, Diener, & Schwarz, 1999). In contrast, from a eudemonic perspective, wellbeing stems from a person's sense of meaning and fulfilment (Ryan & Deci, 2001) and includes social components (Disabato *et al.*, 2016). In recent research (e.g., Mairitsch *et al.*, 2021), wellbeing has been examined from both perspectives, including its social, physical, and psychological dynamic components. In the study presented here, I decided to include both perspectives, seeing wellbeing as it "emerges from the dynamic interplay of personal characteristics and socio-contextual factors" (Mercer, 2021, p. 7).

Studies to date have shown that teacher wellbeing is closely linked to teaching quality and a positive student experience (e.g., Spilt, Koomen, & Thijs, 2011). High levels of stress among teachers can negatively influence relationships with students (Milatz, Lüftenegger, & Schober, 2015), which in turn can contribute to students' deteriorating behaviour and grades (Herman, Reinke, & Eddy, 2020). One way to lower teacher stress and boost wellbeing is to understand the kinds of support they need through their use of coping strategies and how effective they are in diverse situations (Parker *et al.*, 2012).

Coping strategies

The effect of adverse life conditions can be reduced or amplified depending on how an individual copes with stressors and stressful situations (Taylor & Stanton, 2007). Lazarus and Folkman (1984) define coping as "constantly changing cognitive and behavioural efforts to manage specific external and/or internal demands that are appraised as taxing or exceeding the resources of the person" (p. 141). They introduced two types of coping; problem-focused coping, which aims to change the cause of stress, and emotion-focused coping, which aims to reduce emotional distress caused by the stressful situation (Lazarus, 2006). Coping strategies also can be categorised as adaptive and maladaptive (Holton, Barry, & Chaney, 2016). Adaptive coping occurs when coping improves the situation and leads to positive outcomes, such as through seeking social support and exercise, while maladaptive coping strategies may provide a temporary respite but lead to damaging outcomes in the long-term, such as avoiding dealing with the issue, disengaging, or simply ignoring the stressor (Holton *et al.*, 2016). Previous studies on teacher stress showed that using adaptive coping can buffer stressors, whereas relying on maladaptive coping strategies carries a risk of burnout (Skinner & Beers, 2016). Effective coping promotes wellbeing positively as well as reduces distress (Shiota, 2006), and Folkman and Moskowitz (2000) suggested problem-focused coping, creating positive events, and positive reappraisal as predictors of positive wellbeing.

Although opinions differ on how to measure or categorise coping strategies, it is generally agreed that coping strategies are multidimensional and multifunctional (Skinner et al., 2003). Hence, using only one type of coping is rarely sufficient as coping embraces a myriad of actions that an individual can take to manage stressful events. As such, coping is described as an organisational construct rather than one specific behaviour (Skinner et al., 2003; Sideridis, 2006). Skinner et al. (2003) state that individuals' instances of coping are "the countless changing real-time responses people use in dealing with stressful transactions" (p. 248), and these responses reflect the changing and simultaneous nature of using coping strategies. One important implication is that coping strategies must be considered within the context of their use, and not all coping strategies are automatically effective or lead to desirable outcomes (Holton et al., 2016).

Through a longitudinal qualitative study of four language teachers in the context of South Korean universities, this chapter explores what different coping strategies these educators used over time during the first wave of the pandemic and seeks to understand the complex, contextualised, and dynamic nature of their coping processes in their particular teaching contexts.

Teachers in the global pandemic crisis

The World Health Organization declared Covid-19 a pandemic on March 11, 2020. Many countries had to implement measures to minimize face-to-face contacts, such as online/remote learning and teaching (Van Lancker & Parolin, 2020). In many contexts across the globe, teachers were only given short notice to transition from in-person to online teaching, and in many cases, without any prior training or technical support (Reimers et al., 2020).

Several studies have been conducted to date to understand the challenges teachers have faced during the pandemic. For example, Kim and Asbury (2020) explored teachers' experiences of the unexpected change at work and identified six themes of teachers' stories during the first five to six weeks of the outbreak (e.g., uncertainty and reflections). MacIntyre and colleagues (2020) conducted research on language teachers' coping strategies during the pandemic crisis in April 2020. Their findings showed that using avoidant coping, which "tend[s] toward more dysfunctional responses" (e.g., denial and distraction) instead of trying to change or accept the situations, was related to increased stress levels and negative emotions (MacIntyre et al., 2020, p. 3).

The present study

This study aims to understand the experience of four language teachers at universities in South Korea (henceforth Korea) during the Covid-19 pandemic crisis focusing on their perception of stressors and use of coping strategies. In particular, it seeks to answer the following questions: (a) What stressors were experienced by language teachers at universities in Korea during the pandemic crisis? (b) What coping strategies did they use to manage the transition to online teaching?

Context of the study

In Korean universities, teachers were required to adapt to online teaching formats with less than two weeks' notice. On March 2, 2020, the Ministry of Education suggested universities implement distance learning for two weeks. There were no guidelines or suggested methods provided; hence, each university had to decide how to conduct distance teaching and support online classes in a short time. The universities repeatedly delayed getting back to in-person classes until May, when most tertiary institutions announced remote learning for the rest of the semester, until the end of June.

According to the Korean University Professors Association, only 0.92% of courses in 213 Korean universities were conducted online the previous semester, suggesting that most teachers at universities did not have prior online teaching experience (Kim, 2020). For language teachers taking a communicative approach to language teaching, the transition to online teaching posed additional challenges, due to the difficulties in guaranteeing students' active participation in online classes. In contrast to other countries, Korea did not have a lockdown or curfew at that time, meaning there were significant changes for teachers at work but not necessarily in their daily life settings.

Participants

Participants in this study were four English teachers at four Korean universities. Volunteers were recruited through the researcher's personal contacts to facilitate a positive rapport and a greater atmosphere of trust during a sensitive time. Additionally, the participants were recruited from different universities to maximize the diversity of individual experiences in the conversion to distance teaching. The first language of all participants is English, and the participants' demographic information can be found in Table 6.1.

Data collection and analysis

This study draws on two semi-structured interviews and an email journal entry for each participant to provide experiences of distance teaching from the beginning, middle, and end of the spring semester of 2020.

Semi-structured interviews were chosen to understand individuals' experiences in-depth and to compare participants' answers in a specific context over time (O'Leary, 2021). The first interview protocol was comprised of five sections: Personal and professional life in normal circumstances, experiencing the change, coping at work, coping in daily life, and future-self. The second interview sought to explore in-depth issues raised during the first interview, such as changes in the participants' coping strategies, a reflection back on the semester, and their thoughts and emotions at that time. Additionally, each participant provided a voluntary email journal entry with an average of 367 words between the interviews to comment on any ongoing changes in their experiences and thoughts.

The first interviews were conducted in April, the email journal entries were collected in May, and the second interviews were held after the semester in July 2020. All four participants preferred to be interviewed face-to-face. As Korea did not have restrictions or a lockdown, conducting face-to-face interviews was possible, following local safety guidelines. Prior to data collection, confidentiality and anonymity were assured to each participant, and they were informed that they would be able to withdraw from the study at any time before publication. All interviews were audio-recorded and then transcribed for content, including non-verbal expression. To anonymise the data, identifying markers were removed at the point of transcription, and pseudonyms were given to each participant. The study created a total data corpus of 64,194 words.

For data analysis, the transcripts were read repeatedly, and memos were created in MAXQDA 2020. A broad range of categories was identified in light of the research questions through the first round of initial coding, taking a grounded approach (Charmaz, 2006). Next, the data were re-coded inductively under those categories, and a series of themes were created. After identifying the main themes, cycles of open coding were followed to identify sub-themes and components, and connections between codes and groups were checked to see which sub-themes clustered. Then, the list of sub-themes of stressors (e.g., issues with online tools and lack of administrative support) and coping (e.g., seeking support and a sense of accomplishment) was finalized.

Findings

The first part of this section presents the participants' perceived stressors during the conversion to online teaching, and the second part illustrates how they reported coping with those stressors and related frustrations.

Stressors

In exploring how the participants were coping during the pandemic crisis, the participants described stressors they were facing. Three main themes of stressors emerged: Issues with using technology, lack of administrative support, and loss of control in classes.

Table 6.1 *Demographic information of participants*

Pseudonyms	Gender	Years of teaching	Age	Courses	Location of university	Living arrangement	Children
Amy	F	20	46	General English, ESP	Seoul capital area	With a partner	None
Chris	M	15	41	General English	Seoul capital area	With family	2
David	M	12	38	General English, TOEIC, Writing	Outside of Seoul capital area	Commuter family	2
Eric	M	22	50	General English, Writing	Seoul capital area	Alone	None

Issues with using technology

All participants reported that they had not had experience teaching online before; hence, online tools were related to a "fear of the unknown", as Amy described it. Amy and Eric, who were conducting synchronous classes, mentioned that unfamiliarity with the software (e.g., screen sharing and breakout rooms) led to delays during classes. Eric said, "because all this is so new and foreign [unfamiliar tasks and technology], it just seems like so much to keep up with." These teachers reported being concerned about appearing unprofessional to their students as they coped with technological difficulties.

Chris and David, who were conducting asynchronous lessons, reported online system failures caused by overloaded servers. Both of them mentioned having difficulties in uploading teaching materials and errors in students' attendance check-in. In addition, Chris had tried different tools to provide various in-class tasks; nonetheless, he faced technical problems, which could not be fixed in time before his classes, leading to frustration, he explained.

Lack of administrative support

None of the participants knew how long they would have to teach online, as the universities kept announcing and then delaying going back to in-person classes. All participants mentioned the universities' indecisiveness as the biggest cause of stress. For instance, Chris reported that not being able to prepare lessons while having the midterm exams ahead was stressful:

> *They keep doing a delay. "Two weeks later, we're going to start." Two weeks later, "No, we're going to delay again." Because of this, we can't just say, "Let's go ahead and put all our thinking into how to support doing everything online."*

Additionally, all participants pointed out the lack of administrative support. David described the first week of online teaching as "a nightmare" and explained his university's inconsistent instructions: "At the last minute, everything was changed a day before the first class. We had to redo everything." Chris's university instructed teachers to use its learning management software without providing any manuals or training sessions. After the midterms, his university offered a training session for their platform; nevertheless, it got delayed repeatedly and finally did not take place. Chris added, "I have found this semester to be the most tiring semester I have had in my career. Much of this could have been avoided with the training of the system before implementation." A lack of communication and interaction with the administrative office made teachers feel "alone and isolated," as Eric described. He added, "this was a lonely process in many ways."

Amy was the only one who described the university's support positively in the first interview. In her email journal, she wrote that her university was "doing a good job of keeping their teachers informed on things." In the second interview, however, she highlighted the little administrative support received in the end: "It was basically sink or swim. They are good at telling you what you need to do but nothing to help you." The data suggest a mixture of poor communication and an absence of practical support, which together compounded these teachers' experience of stress through the transition to online teaching.

Loss of control in classes

All four teachers reported the loss of control in classes as an issue. Eric said he was frustrated when his students refused to turn their webcams on during synchronous classes, as he felt it damaged the interaction he wanted to have. Similarly, when David tried a synchronous lesson, none of his students wanted to use the microphone; instead, they preferred typing. Chris also highlighted how difficult it was to draw out students' active participation compared to real-time classes.

All participants were aware of the possibility of cheating on exams and their inability to prevent cheating entirely. David added: "The biggest problem with online is doing tests correctly where students can't cheat. That's the most difficult part."

Additionally, all teachers mentioned experiencing access problems with their students' devices, disruptions caused by students' background noise, and technical difficulties on the students' side. Chris commented on the need for solutions and support for students who cannot access technology as easily as other students.

Coping strategies

All participants reported using problem-focused coping strategies primarily at the beginning of the semester. Positive reappraisal appeared to feature consistently as a coping strategy throughout the semester, as showcased in the following sections.

Problem-focused coping

Chris and David adopted a popular messenger application to solve communication problems with their students. Eric asked an assistant to help him record lessons; David tried synchronous classes when he felt the lack of interaction was problematic in asynchronous lessons. Amy and Chris tried to implement various tools (e.g., quizzes) to make their online classes more interactive. However, problem-focused coping was not a significant part of their coping, and it was only reported at the beginning of the semester and with respect to specific technology-induced problems. For example, Chris explained in the second interview that he stopped trying to solve problems around the mid-term period because his attempts to fix problems created a lot of extra work, and he felt that ultimately most problems could not be fixed by him.

Positive reappraisal

Focusing on the positives was the most salient coping strategy used by all the participants throughout the semester, although it was especially notable in the data from the middle of the semester onwards. This type of coping is categorised as positive reappraisal, meaning "a cognitive process through which people focus on the good in what is happening or what has happened" (Folkman & Moskowitz, 2000, p. 115). Especially for coping with teaching online and using technology, data showed that these teachers were conceptualising the conversion to distance teaching as an opportunity for self-development by acquiring new digital skills. Consequently, the sense of achievement from learning to teach online and focusing on the benefits of using technology in teaching appeared to help participants experience positive emotions during this challenging semester.

The participants focused on the positive aspects of working with technology. Eric reported his belief in using video conferencing tools provided the interaction everyone needed during the pandemic crisis. Also, Chris explained that by using different online tools, he could make more student-centred activities and provide various types of support.

In terms of self-development, all teachers had become aware of their own growth, progress, and an increasing sense of self-efficacy. Amy reported that she had learned "to try new things and not stress out if it does not work" and considered upgrading her skills as a benefit of this challenging time. In his second interview, David said that he was considering making an online program, which he could never have imagined doing before, because of his improved skill and confidence in recording lessons. Chris explained that he had learned to accept mistakes and developed "a lot more confidence and a better understanding of how teaching online works." Eric commented that the sudden change to online teaching had forced him to learn new skills and added, "it's given my playbook as a teacher more options to make my classes more interesting and relevant." They all were satisfied with learning how to teach online because they believed that it would be "an essential skill in post-Covid-19 [education]," as Chris highlighted.

For coping in life beyond their online lessons, all participants reported having feelings of gratitude when comparing themselves with others whom they perceived as being worse-off (e.g., people in lockdown). This type of coping strategy is a form of downward social comparison, which appears to support individuals to maintain their perceived wellbeing positively by identifying themselves with others worse-off (Buunk & Dijkstra, 2017). The strategy of downward social comparison was also used in a more holistic sense when all participants expressed feeling lucky to be in a country without a lockdown, especially when they read the news or talked with people in their respective home countries. Additionally, in the second interview, they all compared themselves to other teachers when they expressed their feelings of accomplishment. For example, Chris talked about how other teachers gave fewer assignments to students than he did.

Finally, the data revealed that a sense of the shared experience of "going through the pandemic together" strengthened social connections with their students. For instance, Amy and Eric described that the connections between them and their students were stronger than usual. Through synchronous lessons, the teachers and students could see each other's personal spaces, family members, or pets; Amy said: "I felt that I got really close to them." Eric also commented, "Somehow, I felt more linked to them. I think it was because we were all dealing with the stress of Corona, and I was trying to encourage them."

Discussion

Stressors

Focussing on the negative first, the findings revealed that unfamiliarity with digital tools resulted in a heavy workload and a sense of frustration for the teachers. The uncertainty was exacerbated by universities failing to make decisions and plan for the whole semester. Frustrations arising from last-minute instructions and decisions of the university administration were described because the teachers could not make plans without knowing whether they would continue teaching online. Consequently, the participants reported having a low sense of control in their lessons for the whole semester. We know from other work that a sense of control is tightly connected to wellbeing because of its role as a mediator to reduce negative affect (Jang, Chiriboga & Small, 2008). Therefore, it suggests the importance of ensuring that teachers feel they have a sense of control over their teaching when facing a period of transition.

While the teachers in this study were struggling with technical issues, only psychological and social resources were available for them. Without hands-on support from institutions (e.g., providing clear instructions), it was insufficient to help them cope in practical terms with the technological challenges they were confronted with. This difficulty suggests that accessible and practical resources, such as training and manuals, are crucial for teachers to effectively adapt to educational transitions while promoting wellbeing. To understand levels of wellbeing, Dodge *et al.* (2012) describe the trade-off between the number of challenges faced and the available resources to cope: "When individuals have more challenges than resources, the see-saw dips, along with their wellbeing, and vice-versa" (p. 230). The teachers in the study presented here faced an imbalance at times with greater challenges compared to resources available. However, their use of coping strategies was one way in which they built up and expanded psychological resources to cope despite unresolved practical problems.

Positive reappraisal

While exploring how language teachers were coping with these stressors, positive reappraisal was revealed as a notable coping strategy used by the participants. All four teachers in this study focused on the positives in the conversion to online teaching—reframing the challenging situation as an opportunity for self-development, discovering positive aspects of technology, and feeling grateful by downward social comparisons. Thereby they drew meaning and purpose from their work through feeling more accomplished and connected than in normal circumstances by helping students.

Discovering personal growth opportunities and seeing one's own efforts can benefit other people are forms of positive reappraisal (Folkman & Moskowitz, 2000). Previous research has found a positive association between positive reappraisal, psychosocial wellbeing, and physical health (Moskowitz *et al.*, 2009). Thus, positive reappraisal is suggested as an effective coping strategy because of its ability to increase the experience of positive emotion, which enhances wellbeing (Shiota, 2006). Also, for individuals who experience distress, downward social comparison may increase subjective wellbeing and enhance satisfaction, mood, and optimism (Buunk & Dijkstra, 2017). Drawing meaning and purpose from one's work is known to be a key contributor to wellbeing (Ryan & Deci, 2001). In the conversion to teaching remotely during the pandemic crisis, teachers cannot change the particular situation linked to their stressors. Instead of focusing on things that cannot be changed, focusing on the positives may be the most effective and easily adaptive coping strategy to enhance wellbeing.

Coping and wellbeing over time

In the first interview, negative emotions (e.g., frustration and worry) were expressed by all participants as they shared their stressors and challenges. Problem-focused coping (e.g., changing tools to fix communication problems) was a key coping strategy for all participants, along with downward comparison and positive reappraisal. In the second interview, however, all four participants showed strong positive emotions and referred to positive reappraisal as their primary coping strategy. A reason might be that after adjusting to the situation and facing a sense of helplessness in being unable to solve some of the problems, positive reappraisal became a big part of their coping repertoire (Gray, 2006). In a situation that cannot be altered, problem-solving efforts may cause chronic distress (Lazarus, 1996). As Chris described, attempts to solve problems often led to more stressful situations. Instead, all the participants sought a chance to focus retrospectively on everything that was successfully achieved, which appeared to contribute positively to their wellbeing. A sense of accomplishment at the end of the semester could be another reason they showed strong positive emotions and positive reappraisal (Kern et al., 2015). In addition, previous research in coping strategies revealed that to deal with new challenges, people tend to rely on fewer coping strategies as time passes (e.g., Gray, 2006; Patterson, 2016). Difficulties in online teaching may have become more habitual after a few months, leading to the participants using fewer coping strategies.

The data also showed that teachers' emotions and coping methods changed throughout the semester. This suggests the importance of providing various types of support adequate for the particular stage of a transition or period of change that a teacher may be undergoing. The effects on wellbeing and coping strategies that teachers draw on change and adapt to the ongoing dynamics of a situation; teachers, thus, need different types of support at different moments in time. Ideally, wellbeing is supported in structural terms from institutions as well as through individual coping strategies (Mercer & Gregersen, 2020). On a positive note, however, the teachers in this study displayed resilience in drawing on positive coping strategies, even when institutional and practical technical support was not forthcoming.

Conclusion

This chapter explored the stressors and coping strategies of language teachers during the pandemic crisis based on four examples from Korea. Language teachers' stressors in the conversion to online teaching caused the teachers to have a low sense of efficacy, which affected their wellbeing negatively. Positive reappraisal was revealed to be an effective coping strategy used by these teachers by contributing to maintaining positive emotions. Moreover, since their coping methods appeared to change throughout the semester, the study has highlighted the importance of understanding coping processes over time.

Some limitations of the current study need to be considered. Firstly, Korea did not have a lockdown or restrictions on daily life, so the focus was on the stressors and coping in the workplace. Significant changes in living situations, such as a lockdown, could have revealed different results, with a whole additional range of stressors added to the work-related challenges (MacIntyre *et al.*, 2020). Second, the age range of the participants is from 38 to 50, and teachers in other age groups may show different results. Previous research has indicated that preferences of coping strategies appeared to be varied by age groups; for instance, older people tend to use more emotion-focused coping strategies than younger people (Lazarus, 1996). Further studies inviting researchers and teachers to comment from their experiences is needed to better understand language teachers' experiences during the pandemic crisis.

Implications for the future

The pandemic has highlighted how important teacher wellbeing is in times of crisis. However, less dramatic periods of change can also have an impact on how teachers feel about their work and how they cope with stress. This study suggests valuable implications for supporting teachers in periods of educational transition. The findings draw attention to the need for institutions to improve the support for staff. It is suggested that employers and administrative offices do not have to solve every problem to help teachers; instead, simple interaction and active communication can significantly support teachers in challenging situations. In addition, various types of support can apply to a specific stage of a transition. For instance, at the beginning of the transition to online teaching, guidelines and manuals were critical for the teachers in this study. Providing clear and consistent instructions or training sessions at the beginning would be helpful not only in addressing teachers' practical needs but also in making them feel supported. In the middle of the semester, the teachers were seeking to share their experiences and information. Active communication between the institution and teachers or providing workshops would allow teachers to discuss issues they face. Those may provide them with a sense of belonging and control by sharing their experiences and opinions. Furthermore, providing detailed feedback at the end of the transitioning period would be beneficial for teachers to feel assured of their performance and improve their ways of adapting to the transition for the following semester. Additionally, teachers themselves can become more aware of the importance of looking after their wellbeing by focusing on the positives and aspects within their locus of control rather than on issues they cannot change. Teacher educators should consider introducing and emphasizing positive reappraisal as an effective coping strategy for teachers in difficult times.

Even though this study was conducted in the context of the global pandemic in 2020, its findings have implications for coping under various challenging periods of transition, which happen frequently in education as a result of educational reforms, innovations, or teacher mobility and job changes. It offers insights into how teachers can cope and provides valuable lessons for the wider teaching community as well as the literature on the dynamic nature of coping.

References

Aperribai, L., Cortabarria, L., Aguirre, T., Verche, E., & Borges, Á. (2020). Teacher's physical activity and mental health during lockdown due to the COVID-2019 pandemic. *Frontiers in Psychology, 11*, 2673. https://doi.org/10.3389/fpsyg.2020.577886

Buunk, A. P., & Dijkstra, P. (2017). Social comparisons and well-being. In M. Robinson & M. Eid (Eds.) *The happy mind: Cognitive contributions to well-being* (pp. 311–330). Springer. https://doi.org/10.1007/978-3-319-58763-9_17

Charmaz, K. (2006). *Constructing grounded theory: A practical guide through qualitative analysis*. Sage.

Day, C., & Gu, Q. (2009). Teacher emotions: Wellbeing and effectiveness. In P. A. Schutz & M. Zembylas (Eds.), *Advances in teacher emotion research* (pp. 15–32). Boston: Springer.

Disabato, D. J., Goodman, F. R., Kashdan, T. B., Short, J. L., & Jarden, A. (2016). Different types of well-being? A cross-cultural examination of hedonic and eudaimonic well-being. *Psychological Assessment, 28*(5), 471–482. https://doi.org/10.1037/pas0000209

Dodge, R., Daly, A. P., Huyton, J., & Sanders, L. D. (2012). The challenge of defining wellbeing. *International Journal of Wellbeing, 2*(3), 222–235. https://doi.org/10.5502/ijw.v2i3.4

Folkman, S., & Moskowitz, J. T. (2000). Stress, positive emotion, and coping. *Current Directions in Psychological Science, 9*(4), 115–118. https://doi.org/10.1111/1467-8721.00073

Gray, D. E. (2006). Coping over time: The parents of children with autism. *Journal of Intellectual Disability Research, 50*(12), 970–976. https://doi.org/10.1111/j.1365-2788.2006.00933.x

Herman, K. C., Reinke, W. M., & Eddy, C. L. (2020). Advances in understanding and intervening in teacher stress and coping: The coping-competence-context theory. *Journal of School Psychology, 78*(February), 69–74. https://doi.org/10.1016/j.jsp.2020.01.001

Holton, M. K., Barry, A. E., & Chaney, J. D. (2016). Employee stress management: An examination of adaptive and maladaptive coping strategies on employee health. *Work, 53*(2), 299–305. https://doi.org/103233/WOR-152145

Horwitz, E. K. (1996). Even teachers get the blues: Recognizing and alleviating language teachers' feelings of foreign language anxiety. *Foreign Language Annals*, *29*(3), 365–372. https://doi.org/10.1111/j.1944-9720.1996.tb01248.x

Jang, Y., Chiriboga, D. A., & Small, B. J. (2008). Perceived discrimination and psychological well-being: The mediating and moderating role of sense of control. *The International Journal of Aging and Human Development*, *66*(3), 213–227. https://doi.org/10.2190/AG.66.3.c

Johnson, S., Cooper, C., Cartwright, S., Donald, I., Taylor, P., & Millet, C. (2005). The experience of work-related stress across occupations. *Journal of Managerial Psychology*, *20*(2), 178–187. https://doi.org/10.1108/02683940510579803

Kahneman, D., Diener, E., & Schwarz, N. (Eds.). (1999). *Well-being: Foundations of hedonic psychology*. Russell Sage Foundation.

Kern, M. L., Waters, L. E., Adler, A., & White, M. A. (2015). A multidimensional approach to measuring well-being in students: Application of the PERMA framework. *The Journal of Positive Psychology*, *10*(3), 262–271. https://doi.org/10.1080/17439760.2014.936962

Kim, N. (2020, March 13). 교수들 "화상 수업 해본 적 없어"... 온라인 강의 준비 진땀. https://news.joins.com/article/23729796

Kim, L. E., & Asbury, K. (2020). "Like a rug had been pulled from under you": The impact of COVID-19 on teachers in England during the first six weeks of the UK lockdown. *British Journal of Educational Psychology*, *90*(4), 1062–1083. https://doi.org/10.1111/bjep.12381

Lazarus, R. S. (1996). The role of coping in the emotions and how coping changes over the life course. In *Handbook of emotion, adult development, and aging* (pp. 289–306). Academic Press. https://doi.org/10.1016/b978-012464995-8/50017-0

Lazarus, R. S. (2006). *Stress and emotions: A new synthesis*. Springer.

Lazarus, R. S., & Folkman, S. (1984). *Stress, appraisal, and coping*. Springer.

Luk, J. (2012). Teachers' ambivalence in integrating culture with EFL teaching in Hong Kong. *Language, Culture and Curriculum*, *25*(3), 249–264. https://doi.org/10.1080/07908318.2012.716849

MacIntyre, P. D., Gregersen, T., & Mercer, S. (2020). Language teachers' coping strategies during the Covid-19 conversion to online teaching: Correlations with stress, wellbeing and negative emotions. *System*, 135577. https://doi.org/10.1016/j.system.2020.102352

Mairitsch, A., Babic, S., Mercer, S., Jin, J., Sulis, G., & King, J. (2021). *Being a student, becoming a teacher: The wellbeing of pre-service language teachers in Austria and the UK*. Teaching and Teacher Education, *106*, 103452. https://doi.org/10.1016/j.tate.2021.103452.

Mercer, S. (2020). The wellbeing of language teachers in the private sector: An ecological perspective. *Language Teaching Research*. https://doi.org/10.1177/1362168820973510

Mercer, S. (2021). An agenda for well-being in ELT: An ecological perspective. *ELT Journal*, *75*(1), 14–21. https://doi.org/10.1093/elt/ccaa062

Mercer, S., & Gregersen, T. (2020). *Teacher wellbeing*. Oxford University Press.

Milatz, A., Lüftenegger, M., & Schober, B. (2015). Teachers' relationship closeness with students as a resource for teacher wellbeing: A response surface analytical approach. *Frontiers in Psychology*, *6*, 1–16. https://doi.org/10.3389/fpsyg.2015.01949

Moskowitz, J. T., Hult, J. R., Bussolari, C., & Acree, M. (2009). What works in coping with HIV? A meta-analysis with implications for coping with serious illness. *Psychological Bulletin*, *135*(1), 121–141. https://doi.org/10.1037/a0014210

O'Leary, Z. (2021). *The essential guide to doing your research project*. Sage.

Parker, P. D., Martin, A. J., Colmar, S., & Liem, G. A. (2012). Teachers' workplace well-being: Exploring a process model of goal orientation, coping behavior, engagement, and burnout. *Teaching and Teacher Education*, *28*(4), 503–513. https://doi.org/10.1016/j.tate.2012.01.001

Patterson, G. T. (2016). A brief exploratory report of coping strategies among police recruits during academy training. *Psychological Reports*, *119*(2), 557–567. https://doi.org/10.1177/0033294116662685

Reimers, F., Schleicher, A., Saavedra, J., & Tuominen, S. (2020). Supporting the continuation of teaching and learning during the COVID-19 pandemic. Annotated resources for online learning. *OECD*, 1–38. Retrieved from https://www.oecd.org/education/Supporting-the-continuation-of-teaching-and-learning-during-the-COVID-19-pandemic.pdf

Ryan, R. M., & Deci, E. L. (2001). On happiness and human potentials: A review of research on hedonic and eudaimonic well-being. *Annual Review of Psychology*, *52*, 141–166. https://doi.org/10.1146/annurev.psych.52.1.141

Shiota, M. N. (2006). Silver linings and candles in the dark: Differences among positive coping strategies in predicting subjective well-being. *Emotion*, *6*(2), 335–339. https://doi.org/10.1037/1528-3542.6.2.335

Skinner E., & Beers J. (2016) Mindfulness and teachers' coping in the classroom: A developmental model of teacher stress, coping, and everyday resilience. In K. Schonert-Reichl & R. Roeser (Eds.) *Handbook of mindfulness in education* (pp. 99–118). Springer. https://doi.org/10.1007/978-1-4939-3506-2_7

Skinner, E. A., Edge, K., Altman, J., & Sherwood, H. (2003). Searching for the structure of coping: a review and critique of category systems for classifying ways of coping. *Psychological Bulletin*, *129*(2), 216–269. https://doi.org/10.1037/0033-2909.129.2.216

Sideridis, G. D. (2006). Coping is not an "either" "or": The interaction of coping strategies in regulating affect, arousal and performance. *Stress and Health: Journal of the International Society for the Investigation of Stress*, *22*

(5), 315–327. https://doi.org/10.1002/smi.1114

Spilt, J. L., Koomen, H. M., & Thijs, J. T. (2011). Teacher wellbeing: The importance of teacher–student relationships. *Educational Psychology Review*, *23*(4), 457–477. https://doi.org/10.1007/s10648-011-9170-y

Stickler, U., Hampel, R., & Emke, M. (2020). A developmental framework for online language teaching skills. *Australian Journal of Applied Linguistics*, *3*(1), 133–151. https://doi.org/10.29140/ajal.v3n1.271

Taylor, S. E., & Stanton, A. L. (2007). Coping resources, coping processes, and mental health. *Annual Review of Clinical Psychology*, *3*, 377–401. https://doi.org/10.1146/annurev.clinpsy.3.022806.091520

Van Lancker, W., & Parolin, Z. (2020). COVID-19, school closures, and child poverty: A social crisis in the making. *The Lancet Public Health*, *5*(5), 243–244. https://doi.org/10.1016/S2468-2667(20)30084-0

7
Microblending as a response to Covid-19

David Bish

In the following chapter I will introduce the concept of microblending, where it came from, and what it offers to teachers suddenly teaching online. The chapter then turns to practical advice and examples of microblending in action.

The emergence of microblending: A question of balance

Microblending is the term I coined for a form of teacher-initiated pedagogy I first described in my doctoral research (Bish, 2017). I had noticed this phenomenon emerging in technology enhanced classrooms across an international chain of language schools where I worked as an academic manager. Despite training and scheduled access to a range of technology and electronic materials that matched the syllabus, our teachers did not simply use Information and Communications Technology (ICT) every time it was available. Instead, they made selective use of the technology to get the maximum learning impact. These teachers weren't confining themselves to the rigid structure of our blended learning approach; instead, they were taking control and refining it into something finer—microblending technology to suit their learners' needs.

I realized that these teachers weren't avoiding or refusing the technology as some observers suggest (Selwyn, 2007) or rating technology development rather low (Hämäläinen *et al.*, 2020), but making principled choices about what worked best when. Even more radically, these teachers extended the choice to their students as much as possible, allowing for variation in learner strategies and software in use. This didn't even mean less use of technology: some teachers expanded ICT use beyond classroom time through the flipped classroom or project work on the students' own devices (Bish, 2019).

Microblending is an informed selection of new technology, tempered and framed with techniques from face-to-face teaching. A microblending approach balances a teacher's existing knowledge with technology use.

Microblending in the Covid-19 pandemic

In the Covid-19 pandemic led swing to online learning, I saw the same phenomenon again in the work of some of our best teachers as they moved from physical to virtual classrooms.

While coping with the need to quarantine and isolate students who had travelled abroad as well as offer free lessons to students under lockdown, we asked teachers to run their classes online. Fortunately, we had no shortage of digital tools and an online platform to teach through, but in delivering what had been classroom lessons in an online manner, even teachers with considerable experience with digital technology made sure they struck a balance between what they knew from face-to-face teaching and teaching with technology in a new online space.

I was not alone in observing this, as Justin Reich (2021) reports, under Covid-19 teachers have been "tinkering" with routines they know and finding how technology best fits the learning they want to bring their students to. Reich (2021) suggests in most cases technology alone does not provide learning solutions but that

> millions of teachers have come up with new teaching tricks and classroom routines, and tens of millions of students have deepened their skills in technology-mediated communication and self-regulated learning. (p. 24)

Previously, many authors have cited lack of teacher agency in the integration of technology as to why it does not go well (Selwyn, Dawes, & Mercer, 2001; Bingimlar, 2008), but in the rush to solve problems of the pandemic, teachers have been trusted to help find solutions (Thumvichit, 2021). This is exactly what the microblending teacher does. Epistemologically speaking, this is a constructivist approach (Anderson, 2008; Kaya, 2015) grounded in the thinking of educational theorists such as Piaget, Vygotsky and Bloom which is not unusual in language teachers, who often devise tasks for their own classroom built around the learners and their needs (Gilakjani *et al.*, 2013).

So where do the choices lie in online teaching? At first it might appear that all content must be presented as electronic media and manipulated with electronic tools in a very different type of lesson, nonetheless the teaching within the online classroom can still be humanised. An online classroom is simply a different communication space, and while it is computer mediated communication, the balance of what media is used and how is up to the teacher (Chapelle, 2001).

Teachers need to apply their sense of "plausibility" (Maley, 2018) to what is happening and take more control of the online classroom space. I am not suggesting that teachers should rebel against institutional guidelines, but that they should seek a balance, remembering what worked with these same students in the face-to-face classroom—gestures, eye contact, board work, pronunciation drilling, and so much more I hope to remind readers of below.

Applying what teachers already know

Much of today's approach to teacher training and professional development is built around knowledge models (Hubbard & Levy, 2006). Such models show how, much of what teachers already knew when encountering the pandemic was more useful than many realized. Their knowledge and experience in teaching, coupled with knowledge of the target language and how it is learned seems to equip most teachers with a good foundation to build on for teaching online.

In addition, most teachers will have some degree of knowledge of technology which constantly expands as they encounter new tools. What is also needed, is the skill to critically appraise which technology tools work when, with which students, and in which language teaching context.

As much as a teacher learns to master classroom tools, such as a whiteboard or pronunciation chart, there will also be a learning curve on starting to use an electronic classroom. At first, that is simply learning to use software, in the same way as any businessperson who uses online conference tools in their work does. However, teacher training can overlook that this is actually transforming the way we teach, not simply the tools we use (Hampel & Stickler, 2015), and that making this transformation requires personal critical reflection as teachers adjust what they know about teaching and seek to fit these new tools into their pedagogical beliefs.

As a teacher starts to apply their pedagogic and language knowledge to what they know about software and online resources, they begin to develop what Mishra and Kohler (2006) call TPCK—a new type of Technological Pedagogic Content Knowledge. Much as a teacher may once have thought "I can think of a great way of using that quiz show game in my class," they start to be able to blend technology into their teaching by thinking things like "I could let students use that meme editor to make short presentations."

In a language teacher making the sudden move to online teaching, their language content knowledge and the pedagogical knowledge of how to help students learn can be overlooked. Microblending is about not using technology at the expense of foregoing this knowledge but by retaining balance in managing online classes.

Critical reflection and evaluation

In a pre-pandemic study by Gallardo del Puerto and Gamboa (2009), language teachers reported that the technology available limited their use of the kind of socially interactive learning suggested above. The pandemic has now given teachers access to video conferencing tools that offer the potential for such interaction if thoughtfully used.

A long-recognised trait of effective teaching is the ability to reflect on lessons (Farrell, 2012), considering what worked and what didn't (Tripp, 2011). Effective teachers constantly assess how their material and activities work when teaching and make choices about what to do in upcoming classes to achieve their intended learning outcomes. These outcomes and how to reach them are at least partly in the domain of the student (Ellis, 2006). Those who microblend also consider whether their students can be empowered to make the choice of technology to use. This means both task assessment and considering whether the technology or online media adds anything (Puentadura, 2006). If a non-digital technique can still be used to effect, the technology can be put to one side. For example, when an online teacher I worked with last year saw that 'kale' was being introduced in her next class, she simply took a bag of kale from her kitchen, held it up to the camera and tasted a piece to show it is eaten raw. Using a picture or video may have worked but she had no need to substitute realia with technology and the learners enjoyed the authenticity.

Forgotten choices in online teaching

It is easy to forget that the teacher still has non-tech choices to make about teaching in the online classroom. Many teachers have a wealth of techniques and experience that should not be abandoned just because they are teaching in an online space.

Consider the following checklist of fundamental aspects of teacher craft. This could be used by a teacher in planning, self-reflection or perhaps as a peer observation tool. When moving language teaching online, this checklist can serve as a reminder of elements of classroom teaching to retain online.

A pedagogic self-assessment checklist

- Beginning with a warmer
- Setting context
- Modelling before asking a student
- Grading language and instructions
- Drilling pronunciation
- Redirecting questions to another student
- Concept checking
- Gestures that remind a student to self-correct a known issue
- Student note taking
- Differentiation
- More support for weaker students
- Monitoring silently
- Ensuring every student takes part
- Giving thinking time

- Praising students
- Re-incorporating points from previous lessons
- Using a favourite game or activity students like

Each teacher should draft their own personalised version of this checklist, including techniques that they use in face-to-face classes. This can then be checked both before and after classes, to ensure that the teacher is blending these pedagogic skills with their growing technical skills to reclaim their teaching from the Covid-19 pandemic.

Online materials

One of the first two questions teachers moving online usually ask is "What materials will we use?" The other is typically a request for training, one which this chapter is intended to address. Moving lessons online can create some panic as teachers rush to search for specialist online materials and software tools to teach an "online course," but one of the comforts of microblending is to remember that we already have a considerable amount of material which can be utilised in the virtual classroom in a number of ways.

Simply putting the main lesson aims and stages as a "board menu" onto PowerPoint, Keynote or Google Slides as is often done, is enough to serve as the basis for online materials. This can be enhanced with material from the coursebook or authentic material from the Internet, such as copyright free images and video (search for items with a Creative Commons license). If the teacher has used realia, like restaurant menus, signs, and posters or even business letters in class before, these can now either be held up on camera or photographed, and even turned into editable text with one of the many free web-based Optical Character Recognition (OCR) tools available. Some videoconferencing systems, such as Zoom, also offer wireless connection to a mobile phone either as another class member or as a second input – that then becomes a mobile camera.

Making choices about online materials

On first encountering the online classroom, I have seen many teachers falling into the mode of something like a TV news anchor person, linking segments with talk, possibly breaking into teacher-led discussion, and occasionally showing or 'sharing' their materials one at a time with students. The result is that the students become the audience to all this lesson delivery rather than engaged participants in the class. While orchestrating the online classroom, this kind of teacher-fronted lesson delivery can become the default, if the teacher does not take a step back and consider their options for different ways to work with the material. As Camii West (2021) says:

> Choosing the right blend isn't easy and it will need to be adapted to suit your learner's needs. (p. 12)

Here are some suggestions of alternative ways of handling common materials, based on what I have seen adept microblenders do. This is not intended to be a complete overview but more to uncover some of the classroom dynamics teachers can explore.

Video and audio material

The default option tends to be the teacher showing the video or playing the audio themselves, live in the lesson, sharing it with the class all at the same time. Alternatively, the teacher could send students a link to view the video individually. Here students get more control over what they see and hear. This is the approach typically used in the 'flipped classroom' where students do this in their own time. Nonetheless, it can also work well within class time, providing a psychological break and change of dynamic for the students in moving to individual work at their pace.

As the teacher has very little control of what is going on if students are looking at the material alone, a clear watching task needs to be set. For the students to be listening actively, they need to know what to listen for, be it details or simply their own reactions to the video. Watching a video that is already embedded within the school's online platform or an online extension to course material can provide students with some structure and task instructions while working independently before returning to the classroom at a predetermined time. If it is possible to keep the online classroom or at least text messaging open while this happens, the teacher can also give reminders of the remaining time or information to gather while students work.

Another option is to have groups of students watch all or part of the video together. This can be achieved in breakout rooms or by having students connect to each other in a separate chat. This is excellent for split watching, as what one group hears does not affect another (a real advantage over the physical classroom) but its drawback is the amount of classroom and group management required. Time needs to be spent setting up a task framework before the viewing, ideally involving the students in setting up who will control the video, who will be taking notes and what the overall purpose of their watching is. This may not be a suitable option for younger learners but with some practice and monitoring can empower student groups, especially for example when watching videos created by other student groups.

Website based reading

When selecting a specific learning site, such as for exam practice or one with graded texts, as well as authentic material, such as a news or shopping website, teachers can use the skill of microblending equally well. In microblending, a teacher can extend specialist materials with authentic sites found through a web search that offer genuine functional language practice. Searching for such materials that closely fit the intended learning outcomes of a lesson is often a better use of preparation time than searching for ready-made lessons from other teachers.

Reading a website screenshared online is very demanding as the presenter scrolls back and forth to highlight key points, clicking links and opening new pages. As we all have unique reading strategies, and these are typically what teachers want to build in their learners, it is often better to simply send a link for students to do any reading like this individually.

Students can still be brought together on website-based reading though, maybe to study a particular language feature or earlier in a lesson to point out key aspects of a site before sending students to access it independently. Here, a static screenshare can work well, especially where the teaching platform offers annotation tools to annotate particular areas. This can be done by capturing a key section of such a reading or website layout as an image and sharing it as a slide or pasting it directly to the online whiteboard.

This is also an excellent opportunity to consider giving students control, either when a collaborative whiteboard tool is available or by having a student share screens as they annotate. For example, they may be showing which areas of the text give answers to a comprehension question or pointing out examples of a part of speech. The clear example text and their annotations, which might be the outcome of earlier groupwork, serve to scaffold productive skills and language focused explanations building learner confidence and strategies.

Student writing as material

In the online classroom, anything a student writes becomes readily accessible to the teacher and fellow students. Even early on in online lessons, students will begin choosing to interact with the teacher and others through text chat. This often adds to the fluency and range of their classroom language from greetings to clarification requests which serve both as a model to other students and as a part of the lesson transcript for later reference. This communication strategy can be capitalised on by the teacher to encourage more L1 use and as a bridge to more extended writing.

I will now provide three examples for student writing that I have seen teachers explore in their online classes.

The first example is a classroom discussion which took place purely as text chat. This text could be returned to, corrected or edited later.

In the second example a piece of writing was composed using the classroom whiteboard tool. Here, the teacher or a student can act as the sole "scribe" or note-taker for the group while others verbally point out corrections or annotations. This type of classroom management presents a challenging role for a stronger student in the class allowing for differentiation. Depending on the platform used, it may also be possible to have multiple students writing or annotating at the same time. This is much like the brainstorming or group writing games many teachers have students do at the whiteboard in the physical classroom but if this activity is performed online, the text becomes easier to move around, copy and paste or edit to correct.

In the third example a longer piece of writing was written by each student on their own word processor. With this activity a teacher might start students off with a title or opening paragraph simply by pasting it to them in the text chat or onscreen notes. This individual writing may be completed between meetings or as a break of pace in a longer class where the student has the chance to disconnect from others for a moment and focus on their own work. Writing of this sort can be sent to the teacher to correct, to another student to read and respond to, or as something that will be re-edited in a later stage of the lesson.

Some teachers advocate getting fully interactive with a text using a collaborative editor, such as Google Docs. In this app, every student in the class or group can work on the text at the same time with their contributions clearly marked. If a document like this is open at the same time as voice chat, students can explain and make their edits to a document together prompting the "think aloud" type of interaction that we look for in pair work in a physical classroom.

Finally, thinking low-tech, there is still the option of students writing on pieces of paper and uploading a screenshot of these to share with the class. These screenshots can also be pasted to the whiteboard for corrections and discussion using the whiteboard tools.

Coursebook material

While most published English as a Foreign Language (EFL) coursebooks have companion websites or an electronic version for interactive whiteboard use which can be utilised in the lesson in ways suggested above, there is still the print copy of the coursebook which will be in many students' hands before, during or after online lessons. The teacher shouldn't disregard this valuable offline resource and consider how taking the choice to work off the screen is valid in terms of varying student focus, lesson intensity and tempo. For teachers having to cover more time with online lessons replacing previously face-to-face ones, focused coursebook work can provide an effective psychological break to the online class format.

As I have suggested before, a possible choice is to leave the class messaging open while students work from their coursebook or have them connect in breakout rooms so that students can check and compare thoughts together. Where such groupwork is more task-based, the outcomes can be reported back when the whole class has come back together.

An important pedagogical aspect of working with the coursebook is that students typically write answers and notes in the book, changing the focus from screen time and giving them something to look back on offline. With younger students this also gives them something which may be shared with parents as evidence of progress or to show that homework has been completed.

Webtools and apps

Teacher training pre-pandemic introduced many of us to a variety of tools and apps both for learning, such as the plethora of flashcard and quiz making tools, and those designed specifically for aspects of language study like pronunciation apps. These are supplemented by tools like grammar correctors, dictionaries, and translation apps that any language user may find useful. In microblending, teachers consider how these can extend learning beyond the classroom and give a balance of individual focus time to a whole-group class where there is a danger that students remain passive. Many of these tools and apps work well for different individuals and can be integrated into a lesson, especially those which connect students or their work in some way, such as building a set of revision quizzes or even singing together in English with a karaoke app.

A teacher is likely to come across apps they feel are useful and those they think are not. In this context, a microblending perspective offers two key considerations:
1. Enabling learners to make choices of learning tools that work for them. These choices may be guided by recommendations from their peers, and they in turn should be encouraged to share what works for them and keeps them engaged with their learning.
2. While no teacher will know every app or online tool out there, critically applying their pedagogic knowledge to any tool encountered enables an evaluation of how it can constructively contribute to language learning. Teachers need to consider whether this would be through students' independent use or integrated into a class either live or as offline self-study or project work.

When a tool does fit the classroom, teachers and students pass on word and there is a rapid craze of adoption as happened pre-pandemic with Quizlet (a group flashcard and quizzing tool) and Kahoot! (an interactive quiz tool). What the true microblending teacher will know is when the tool is being used as apparent novelty with little pedagogic gain, or when it is no longer suitable, and it is just being used out of habit. The teacher should also consider avoiding any free tools which expose students to unwelcome advertising or require them to share personal data.

Lesson planning

In selecting what to use when, the microblending teacher is making many decisions themselves on lesson planning and execution in the so-called 'bricolage' (Hatton, 1988) of constructing a lesson. This constructivist approach recognises that the format of lessons should vary as they bring together the learners, resources and the teacher to reach the intended learning outcomes.

Microblending requires giving attention to the stages of a lesson, each of which may need more or less technological facilitation, and which may be altered, moved or removed. I have seen many teachers fail to consider the question "Just because it's the next slide in the PowerPoint presentation, do we have to do it?" and their rich and student-centred lesson suddenly becomes linear and predictable. Any teacher who avoids lessons that simply work through each coursebook activity in turn will know how much more fulfilling a lesson can be where they sequence the elements to suit their group, avoiding less challenging activities and supplementing with authentic or specialist material as needed.

Constructing a lesson

Working with the materials and tips above can provide either smaller practice tasks or the main task of a microblended lesson but other valuable elements of a communicative lesson should not be forgotten. In following a 'bricolage' or 'pick and mix' approach to constructing a lesson the stages in a teacher's usual lesson format can still be followed, considering how to best use the technology in each stage separately.

While a microblending mindset can be applied to any lesson planning framework, it seems particularly well suited to a task-based lesson (Willis & Willis, 2007), structured on an Engage, Study, Activate (ESA) stage model (Harmer, 2007). Here are some suggestions of the type of work that could fit into each stage.

Engage – Warmer activities

The purpose of the warmer activities described in this section is to activate the students' language knowledge and to connect it with the theme of the lesson.

Coursebook-based lessons often achieve engagement and connection through pictures or a question or two to consider the lesson theme. This idea can be extended by playing a short video clip or showing a GIF (an animated picture) that contains or suggests the lesson language point for students to guess. The teacher can make this more immersive by using a different image as a virtual background and beginning by asking the students where they are today. Students can then find a similar image to "go there" too.

Teachers can also start with an opinion question, such as 'When is the best time to go on holiday?' and offer a choice of answers using a polling tool or simply the reaction icons on the teaching platform. This makes a good lead into a follow up question for students who voted a particular way.

As many online teachers are working from home, there is often plenty of realia that can be used for setting the scene for a lesson like a jar of cookies, a wine glass, or more smart or casual clothes that can foster a uniquely personal connection with the students and start a fun guessing game. As an extension, students can even join in, for example by starting the lesson with each bringing a favourite book or treasured possession to the lesson and briefly saying why.

Classroom speaking warmers still work online with microphones open, for example by sending one student a word in a private text message (I call this 'whispering') and giving the group 20 yes/no questions to guess the word. The exception is name games, as names now helpfully appear on screen, but students can still share fun facts about one another to remember in memory games.

Text chat activities can make a gentle start to some speaking games, such as using a word snake where students successively add new words beginning with the last letter from the previous word. Another activity is playing vocabulary tennis, where teams go back and forth adding a word in the theme until one team is too slow.

Study – Language focus and practice activities

Above, I have already detailed ways for exploiting different input material. Here are some options for presenting through an online platform.

In an online class quality "board work" that can be prepared in advance, such as substitution tables, short model texts and timelines. Using a degree of animation to build up the table or colour the text, one click at a time, can enhance these presentations.

Any such presentations can also be "flipped," giving the students—individuals or groups—the responsibility of putting key language input on the board and explaining concepts to others. Teachers may have to build up to this or give support, such as checking in with groups preparing to present a point. Nonetheless, learner engagement and attention can increase significantly, especially with ESP (English for Special Purposes) or EAP (English for Academic Purposes) groups, or even when teaching students one-to-one.

Polls make an excellent tool for the closed questions needed in concept checking. Teachers should prepare some common ones in advance like yes/no or numbers, or by creating specific items live and have all students vote on what they think is the answer. Initially hiding student responses will show the teacher how much has been understood before revealing the responses to the class and following up as needed.

Activate – Language use tasks

Here, the aim is to have students actively involved using the target language naturally. Ideally, turn taking activities in larger classes should be avoided; instead, teachers might consider tasks where students can work together. This can often be facilitated by breakout rooms where groups work together on a task before coming back to report on it.

Another way to compensate for the difficulties of getting all students involved is to use an authentic formal structure like a courtroom, debate, or board meeting format where students can be assigned roles including those monitoring language. Extending this setting can have some groups preparing or monitoring while others are speaking or responding. These 'role stations' can be rotated, keeping all students engaged on an aspect of the larger task.

If students are working in larger groups, a teacher can still provide individual input and support by "whispering" to an individual through the text chat for corrections or suggestions.

Where a recording or automatically generated transcript is available on the platform (recordings can be more intimidating for students, especially teens), this can be used to reflect on accuracy or use of the target language. This can also provide a basic draft for follow up writing, bearing in mind that automated transcriptions are not word perfect, so there will be plenty of language to improve.

Using a task-based or problem-solving approach, students are often creating something in the main task, such as a business plan, a brochure or presentation. Collaborating on such work with tools such as Google Docs (a collaborative word processor) or Slides (collaborative presentation software) is authentic and meaningful.

Aside from live collaboration, groups can work together on documents including recordings or videos they share with classmates via a class Dropbox. In the same way, a group can build up a set of multimedia flashcards with a tool, such as Chegg Prep or Quizlet, that can be used to train and test classmates.

Lesson closure – Focus on learning outcomes

Technically, in ESA this is simply another "study" phase but one that should not be neglected in the move to online teaching. I have seen several teachers use final summary and reflection techniques taken directly from their face-to-face teaching to effectively close online lessons. Ideally, the students actively contribute to this final focus on what they have learned; online examples include taking polls, group whiteboard writing or a text chat activity to make a visual record for later reference.

Final thoughts

This chapter has described how "microblending"—an informed selection of new technology, tempered and framed with techniques from their face-to-face teaching—has helped some teachers who were forced to move online due to the Covid-19 pandemic to find a positive way forward.

The emerging strategies of microblending are detailed as ways to counterbalance the disruption of the switch to online teaching and learning. They allow experienced language teachers to build on their pedagogic expertise and their already existing technological knowledge to make informed adaptations in the online classroom. This produces grounded learning opportunities for students. Underlying this incremental adoption of online tools and tasks is an epistemology of constructivist lesson creation. To help teachers critically appraise aspects of the lesson planning, a self-assessment checklist along with examples of a microblended approach to the use of online materials, tools and platforms have been presented. Drawing the theoretical and practical material together, the chapter closes with an outline of planning options for online English lessons. Rather than a prescriptive and linear framework for classroom practice, this chapter presents a description of the creative choices a teacher can make when microblending.

While the pandemic has resulted in a huge shift in the amount of technology teachers and learners need to navigate in online lessons, it has also given teachers new opportunities to selectively use the technology tools of the online classroom to facilitate and enhance teaching. These experiences will influence language teaching well beyond the pandemic.

Perhaps more than ever, teachers are being relied on, trusted, and listened to by their institutions. This puts teachers in a position where they can affect their own classroom pedagogy, one that suits their learners and context. I believe that teacher agency has possibly never been higher than in the pandemic, with many institutions relaxing expectations of formulaic teaching, removing regular testing and demand for constant learner progress, even ceasing observations of classes, all resulting in refreshing autonomy and empowerment for teachers (Damşa *et al.*, 2021).

The suggestions to microblend technology with what teachers know of effective classroom practice offers a way out from blanket adoption of a hurriedly assembled plethora of online media and tools intended to keep learners occupied. Switching from a monitoring or caretaker role to that of a microblender offers teachers a chance to drive learning forward and avoid the "learning loss" (Dorn *et al.*, 2021) many feared in the pandemic. This chapter has presented several examples of genuine pedagogic innovation online teaching offers (such as using media at students own pace, collaborative editing, the use of transcripts and more); however, principled and judicious use of such innovations alongside established routines of effective teaching is now in the province of the teacher. I hope some of the ideas presented in this chapter have been useful or, if not, that in considering them, teachers might discover even better ways to microblend technology into their personal teaching style.

References

Anderson, T. (Ed.). (2008). *The theory and practice of online learning*. Athabasca University Press.

Bingimlas, K. A. (2008). Barriers to the successful integration of ICT in teaching and learning environments: A review of the literature. *Eurasia Journal of Mathematics, Science & Technology Education*, 2009, 5(3), 235–245.

Bish, D. W. (2017). *Increasing the impact of ICT in language learning: Investigating the effect of teachers' ownership of microblending CALL in the classroom within the WST model of ICT use.* https://ore.exeter.ac.uk/repository/handle/10871/33190

Bish, D. W. (2019, April 11-13). Microblending: the effective use of technology in the language classroom [Conference presentation]. *EAQUALS International Conference 2019, Madrid, Spain.*

Chapelle, C. A. (2001). *Computer applications in second language acquisition.* Cambridge University Press.

Damşa, C., Langford, M., Uehara, D., & Scherer, R. (2021). Teachers' agency and online education in times of crisis. *Computers in Human Behavior, 121,* 106793.

Dorn, E., Hancock, B., Sarakatsannis, J., & Viruleg, E. (2021). *Covid-19 and education: The lingering effects of unfinished learning.* McKinsey & Company. https://mckinsey.com/industries/education/our-insights/Covid-19-and-education-the-lingering-effects-of-unfinished-learning

Ellis, R. (2006). The methodology of task-based teaching. *Asian EFL Journal, 8*(3).

Farrell, T. S. (2012). Reflecting on reflective practice: (Re)visiting Dewey and Schon. *TESOL Journal, 3*(1), 7–16.

Gallardo del Puerto, F., & Gamboa, E. (2009). The evaluation of computer-mediated technology by second language teachers: Collaboration and interaction in CALL. *Educational Media International,* 46(2), 137–152.

Gilakjani, A. P., Leong, L. M., & Ismail, H. N. (2013). Teachers' use of technology and constructivism. *International Journal of Modern Education & Computer Science,* 5(4), 49–63.

Hämäläinen, R., Nissinen, K., Mannonen, J., Lämsä, J., Leino, K., & Taajamo, M. (2021). Understanding teaching professionals' digital competence: What do PIAAC and TALIS reveal about technology-related skills, attitudes, and knowledge? *Computers in Human Behavior, 117,* 106672. 1–17.

Hampel, R. & Stickler, U. (Eds.) (2015). *Developing online language teaching: Research-based pedagogies and reflective practices.* Springer.

Harmer, J. (2007). *How to teach English* (2nd ed.). Longman.

Hatton, E. J. (1988). Teachers' work as bricolage: Implications for teacher education. *British Journal of Sociology of Education,* 9(3), 337–357.

Hubbard, P., & Levy, M. (Eds) (2006). *Teacher education in CALL.* John Benjamins Publishing.

Kaya, H. (2015). Blending technology with constructivism: Implications for an ELT classroom. *Teaching English with Technology, 15*(1), 3–13.

Maley, A. (2018). The teacher's sense of plausibility. *Training, Language and Culture, 2*(1), 23–37.

Mishra, P., & Koehler, M. J. (2006). Technological pedagogical content knowledge: A framework for teacher knowledge. *Teachers College Record, 108*(6), 1017-1054.

Puentedura, R. R. (2006). *Transformation, technology, and education.* http://hippasus.com/resources/tte/

Reich, J. (2021). Ed tech's failure during the pandemic, and what comes after. *Phi Delta Kappan, 102*(6), 20–24.

Selwyn, N. (2007). The use of computer technology in university teaching and learning: a critical perspective. *Journal of Computer Assisted Learning,* 23. 83–94.

Selwyn, N., Dawes, L. & Mercer, N. (2001). Promoting Mr. Chips: the construction of the teacher/computer relationship in educational advertising. *Teaching and Teacher Education, 17,* 3–14.

Thumvichit, A. (2021). English language teaching in times of crisis: teacher agency in response to the pandemic-forced online education. *Teaching English with Technology,* 21(2), 14-37.

Tripp, D. (2011). *Critical incidents in teaching: Developing professional judgement.* Taylor & Francis.

West, C. (2021). Blended learning: the past, present and future. *IATEFL Voices, 282,* 12–13.

Willis, D., & Willis, J. (2007). *Doing task-based teaching.* Oxford University Press.

8
Collaborative conclusion

Ursula Stickler and Martina Emke and all authors

The motivation

Teaching online and with technology is challenging for language teachers, and this situation has been exacerbated in the wake of the Covid-19 pandemic. However, language teachers have found creative and collaborative ways to meet the challenges they are faced with in their teaching. We hope that the variety of approaches described in this book will help language teachers to develop their own creative pedagogies and to become more resilient and better equipped to deal with constraints—and sometimes crises—that affect them and their teaching. For researchers, this book offers insight into the language education research that has been carried out during the Covid-19 pandemic and into some of the issues that deserve further exploration, for instance in the areas of teacher professional development and teacher wellbeing.

The gap

In parallel to the experience of many language teachers during the pandemic, teacher trainers and researchers also found their work one of solitary efforts. However, this feeling of solitude was at odds with the desire to exchange experiences, find commonalities, and reassurances. While editing this book, we learnt that our authors - like other researchers - struggled with various pressures: the need to help teachers, the expectations to collect data and publish quickly.

Collaboration often was left behind. This chapter was a deliberate effort to allow all our authors and contributors to take a step back, to consider their own position and the contributions of others to this book.

The process

Straying from the traditional way of writing a summative final chapter, the editors decided to invite all authors to contribute to a collaborative text, based on questions which were designed to encourage reflective writing. The collaborative and iterative asynchronous writing process, during which the final chapter was created, started by the two editors reading all individual chapters separately, looking for overarching themes which could be addressed in the form of questions. The resulting seven questions, together with some instructions, were transferred to to a Google document a link to which was then sent to the authors. As part of this initial stage all authors were also provided with the chapter from another contributor to the book, with two authors asking to be sent more chapters. The authors provided their texts on the Google document within one month; since the authors wrote at different times, not all authors could see everyone's contributions.

The result

The collaborative, asynchronous writing resulted in a virtual dialogue. Encouraged to take a look at other chapters, the authors reflect on their research, their place within the language teaching research and staff development community, and comment on their and others' contributions. Having read all contributions, the editors decided to integrate the answers to the seventh question, which refers to the book series at large, in the introduction.

How we present it

Without taking away the dialogic process and hiding individual contributor's voices, we decided to edit only very slightly, keeping the order of questions and contributions intact. This text, the current framing, happened after the collection of authors' contributions. Table 8.1 (see below) shows the authors identified by their names and initials in the order they contributed to the Google document. What follows next is in the original lay-out: our instructions to contributors and our questions were presented first. In the text below the questions, the order of the contributions and the original texts are maintained as much as possible. This explains that later contributions can refer to earlier text but not the other way around.

Instructions for authors

Below we have drafted seven questions that should guide the structure of our concluding chapter.

As editors, we will write the introduction, explain the process of writing together, and (very gently) edit the contributions. We will NOT change your opinion or voice :-) We will also add our own responses to the questions. We will start the final editing AFTER the writing process has been completed.

- First of all, please enter your name and initials in the list of authors.
- For each point below (1 to 7), please pick the sub-question variant

Table 8.1 *List of authors in the order they contributed (temporal rank order)*

Name	Initials	Author of Chapter
Pauline Ernest	PE	2
Jackie Robbins	JR	4
Aline Germain-Rutherford	AGR	3
Banafsheh Karamifar	BK	3
Tomáš Klinka	TK	3
Sun Shin	SS	6
Joseph Hopkins	JH	4
Hélène Pulker	HP	5
Karina von Lindeiner-Stráský	KvLS	5
Elodie Vialleton	EV	5
Sarah Heiser	SH	2
David Bish	DB	7

which applies best to your book chapter. Answer as fully as you can, with a suggested upper word limit of 250 words per question.
- Please set your initials BEFORE your contributions. Separate your writing from others by starting a new paragraph. If you work(ed) in an authoring team, feel free to add your individual responses OR work together as a team to author your responses.
- Dates and deadlines: The document will remain open until 30 March to enter your responses. You can come back and edit your OWN response as often as you want but only up until 30 March.
- We will be monitoring entries in the meantime. Drop us a line if you have any problems with the Google doc.

As this is a new way of writing a collaborative chapter, we are very excited and looking forward to it :-)

1
What inspired you to design and facilitate a teacher professional development offer in response to the pandemic challenges you / your colleagues / other teachers were presented with? What inspired your research?

PE: During the pandemic, academic communities worldwide responded to the challenges faced by teachers with a wide and inspiring array of professional development initiatives offering support and practical assistance. We felt it was important to provide an analysis of a selection of these, not only because we thought they might be useful for teachers and researchers in the short term, but also because, in the longer term, we hoped they would provide a basis for reflection and integration of new skills and resources which could benefit teachers in their regular professional practice.

JR: At our institution, where we have teachers from a wide range of teaching backgrounds: in terms of countries, teaching institutions (private and public), student profiles (secondary, university, language schools), we were hearing that teachers were struggling a great deal to move their teaching online with minimal training (if any). As part of the ICT-REV team, we were confident we could offer help, at least with offering a curated selection of tools and resources. As we explain in our chapter, the idea of offering some kind of online training came up in a meeting with the ICT-REV team.

SS: I witnessed my colleagues' frustration in having to quickly adapt to online teaching while guiding students through it. Most teachers did not have any experience teaching online but tried figuring it out by searching for information on the internet or asking other teachers. Whether online teaching was something completely new and scary or familiar and manageable, teachers sought opportunities to share information, feelings, and experiences. I decided to conduct this study to help them share their valuable experiences, make them feel supported, and remind ourselves—the stakeholders—of what teachers were going through and what could help them in this type of emergency educational transition.

AGR: In my role as an academic administrator at my institution, whose portfolio also includes the teaching and learning support service for teachers, it was my responsibility to ensure that the online courses that professors had to develop quickly were able to provide a sound online learning experience for students. It was therefore necessary to expand, strengthen and broaden the pedagogical support structure for all faculty in the institution. But it was also essential to measure the effectiveness and impact of the various forms of professional development and the many pedagogical and technological resources developed, both on the online teaching experience of the faculty and on the online learning experience of the students. My office therefore decided to undertake a longitudinal study from the spring of 2020 (the beginning of the pandemic) to the end of winter 2021 (when preparations for the return to campus began), by means of three surveys conducted each trimester during the year, and addressed to all faculty members of the institution, all teaching assistants, and all and then a representative sample of students. The results of these surveys, which addressed not only the pedagogical and technological aspects of online teaching and learning, but also mental health and wellness issues, allowed us to monitor the challenges, successes and needs expressed, in order to adjust as quickly as possible to the pedagogical, technological and mental health support offered to faculty and students.

JH: I think what inspired us most was seeing teachers struggling to come to grips with having to switch literally overnight to online teaching and, as experts in this area, wanting to do anything we could to help. I believe a willingness to pitch in is actually quite a natural reaction in any crisis situation. Another motivating factor for us was to try something completely new, and that's exactly what we did by organizing what turned out to be a massive online event via YouTube Live and, in spite of the huge number of attendees, we were able to maintain a certain degree of interactivity. In terms of research, we didn't actually give this much thought at the time, but then afterwards it became clear that many people could benefit from our experience and so, therefore, it needed to be documented.

HP+KvLS+EV: At the start of the lockdowns in Europe, we witnessed privately how teachers were struggling. For example, we saw this as parents, supervising our children's online schooling. We also saw this through colleagues and friends, in the UK and beyond, who were contacting us, as experienced distance and online language teachers and researchers, for advice and help. Several of us perceived the sense of an urgent need to assist colleagues, and quickly designed a Toolkit to offer support.

SH: With the experience of Open and Distance Learning as the tuition model at the Open University UK and having designed and conducted a fair amount of professional development for the part-time tutors, when the pandemic forced everyone online, it felt like it was correct to help. With the ICT-REV team I was involved in the webcast we offered via the ECML YouTube channel and similarly with the chapter, the offering is strengthened by working with colleagues from other distance learning providers. We have similar but distinct experiences. The public health emergency with people staying home in part to protect each other may well have been an intensifier for relevant professionals wishing to share in a timely manner. Certainly, in the writings reviewed in our chapter, this seemed to have been the case, with many also seeking to use their experience to plan for similar future scenarios.

DB: My research stems from direct observations of online classes in supporting teacher development and in that respect is much like the teacher stories HP+KvLS+EV mention. In earlier work I had also come across the unsettling effect of lack of control mentioned by Sun Shin (Chapter 6).

While some schools cut back on teacher observations during the pandemic, for us it was important as ever when numbers of online classes increased to ensure quality in teaching. We set up a buddy system of peer observations for teachers new to online teaching and I was impressed to see flashes of brilliance from those who came online for the first time during the pandemic with their innovative 'tinkering' with how to present a lesson. For many more, then and even now in online observations I find teachers newly adopting technology believing that it has nothing to do with the classroom teaching they managed before. Here I am striving to help teachers see that what they already know can be relevant in this new space.

2
Where do you see your voice / your contribution in the landscape of moving language teachers online during and after the pandemic? What is your preferred medium / voice / format? How did / does / will your work help teachers prepare for the future?

PE: Some aspects of the professional development initiatives that we examined had emerged in immediate response to the pandemic and were of specific relevance to that situation. However, many significant issues also emerged which are equally applicable to regular (i.e., non-pandemic related) blended/hybrid or fully online language courses. We hope that lessons learnt can become an integral part of future training initiatives.

JR: We hope that our chapter can help other training programmes to make the shift from face-to-face workshops to larger webinar formats. The pandemic has encouraged institutions to offer teacher development to participants based in different places. This has positive implications for sustainable development goals too, namely quality education (through increased training opportunities), reduced inequality (those teachers who cannot afford to travel can still take part), responsible consumption and production (less travel reduces costs), and climate action (less travel means less impact on the climate). All of these points are also relevant for teachers moving their language teaching online after the pandemic. My aim is to continue researching the opportunities that online language education (and training) provides.

SS: Through the chapter, I wanted to tell teachers who have been struggling that they were not alone by sharing others' experiences of the transition and how they tried making online teaching happen smoothly. I'd also like to raise stakeholders' awareness about how to support teachers for any sudden transitions in any educational form, especially regarding the importance of communication and interactions.

AGR: In our chapter we have tried to address a concern, or perception, often relayed by students and instructors who suddenly found themselves in a new and, for many, unusual teaching and learning environment: a sense of solitude in an environment dominated by the notion of distance. We felt it was important to help instructors to understand this concept better, to become familiar with it, to put it into perspective and to link it to the notions of presence and proximity, in order to transform this sometimes painful experience of teaching and learning online into an engaging and inspiring pedagogical experience.

JH: I believe that our chapter could help trainers to design online teacher development events designed to reach much larger audiences than traditional face-to-face workshops, at least in terms of content delivery. The challenge still remains how to provide attendees with opportunities to use that content to design learning activities for students, to share ideas/experiences with other colleagues, which is much more feasible in smaller-scale events.

HP+KvLS+EV: Our instinct was to work within our Higher Education community in the first instance at least. We did this by seeking support from the University Council of Modern Languages in the UK and, through them, reaching out more widely to language practitioners in the UK HE community. We firstly designed the toolkit to share our own teaching voice, and then offered online workshops to give language teachers an opportunity to voice their own concerns, discuss their own experience and share tips. Through this, we provided a platform for the discussion of emerging good practice early on in the pandemic.

SH: The lessons learnt through the rapid adaptations that we reviewed showed an aspiration for many to plan for the future. This was the case both for authors already involved in teaching languages online and those new to it, identifying as a benefit to have had the push to engage with internet-based ways of working that might in the future complement their long-established skills.

DB: Dissemination is always a challenge and although webinars, blogs and vlogs seem to be a natural response given teachers' current state of connectedness, we have to guard against "Zoom fatigue." A coursebook author I know recently lamented in a post: "Not another webinar about giving online trainings about online teaching!"

For me, while open source online media offer practitioners accessible and readily applicable techniques, there is a need to reach teacher trainers and institutions with frameworks for training, teacher observation and reflection. Only by engaging with what actually happens in the online classroom and scrutinising it, can we help teachers develop professionally through reflective practice.

3
How does your chapter compare / contrast to other issues discussed in the book? How do you make a link to other chapters?

PE: We mention training initiatives offered by the Open University UK and the European Centre for Modern Languages ECML, which are discussed in more detail in other chapters in the book.

JR: We refer to the ICT-REV Training and Consultancy programme at the ECML, which is discussed in other chapters. There are also strong links between our chapter and another, which goes into depth about the concept of distance and proximity in online education (Chapter 3). This was one of the principal challenges we faced in carrying out our webinar: encouraging participants to feel involved in the webinar.

SS: The chapter explores an in-depth example of language teachers' experiences during the emergency transition to online teaching. These examples may not represent most teachers' experiences. However, sharing detailed experiences of a particular group of language teachers supports making connections with other chapters to fill in a wide picture of what language teachers need.

AGR: As Jackie Robbins says, we refer to the ICT-REV Training and Consultancy programme at the ECML, which is discussed in other chapters. We also see some links with the teaching strategies and sample activities proposed in Chapter 7 on the concept of Microblending. Our chapter provides the theoretical framework for these proposed strategies, especially with regard to the dimensions of pedagogical presence and socio-cognitive presence.

JH: I found that the concepts of distance, proximity, and presence, presented in Chapter 3, provided a nice theoretical complement to our chapter, which had a much more practical focus. Similarly, our chapter (Chapter 4), which focused on an experience of teacher trainers, is complemented well by Pauline Ernest and Sarah Heiser's chapter (Chapter 2), which highlighted various experiences in Emergency Remote Teaching (ERT) from a teacher's perspective.

HP+KvLS+EV: There are several common threads in our Chapter and Chapter 4, which present two different initiatives and resources addressing the same need to support language teachers to transition to online teaching. Both projects aimed to boost teachers' confidence and skills, and to provide them with an opportunity to reflect on their experiences. The two chapters are testimony that experienced online language practitioners and researchers stepped up to help out their colleagues in a time of crisis. They both suggest that interventions such as the toolkit

(Chapter 5) and the webinars (Chapter 4) were effective in supporting teachers at the start of the crisis.

Although the authors of the two chapters make use of different research questions, frameworks and methodologies, the research presented is underpinned by similar pedagogic principles (e.g. the integration of technology and pedagogy, learner-centredness, teachers as facilitators). Common ideas and findings also emerge from the two chapters. For example, both sets of authors highlight the necessity and usefulness of specific teacher training on online language teaching. Questions are raised about whether this should focus more on pedagogy or on technology, and on whether the two things are inseparable. The notion of teacher confidence is another common theme in the chapters. Both chapters report that teachers focussed on building a sense of community for their students when their teaching moved online; the toolkit team (Chapter 5) indeed found that teachers were much more focused on their students' wellbeing and creating a sense of belonging for them while teaching online. The conclusions in Chapter 4 focus on the integration of large-scale online training into more local and small training events to foster collaboration between specific groups of teachers. Chapter 5 also concludes on the importance of communities of practice for language teachers to develop their skills and confidence to teach online.

SH: As the initial chapter, ours is a review of international reflections of language teachers adapting rapidly for the new restrictions and the help, typically on websites, provided by institutions and umbrella organisations. There is a particular link with the chapters where the authors present in detail the activities, they provided to the language teaching community as a whole, whether synchronously or asynchronously.

DB: The microblending chapter is grounded in what I have observed in online classes as does the opening chapter from Pauline Ernest and Sarah Heiser (Chapter 2) and Sun Shin's exploration of teacher stories (Chapter 6). Rather than deconstructing the teacher's malaise, I see the real benefit of my chapter (Chapter 7) in the practical support I present. The routines and techniques I offer can be viewed effectively in the light of the theoretical framework mentioned in Aline Germain Rutherford, Banafsheh Karamifar and Tomáš Klinka's chapter (3) and complements the toolkits from Hélène Pulker, Karina von Lindeiner-Stráský and Elodie Vialleton (Chapter 5).

Under loss of control in the classroom (Chapter 6) Sun Shin highlights how in the sudden shift online students showed greater familiarity with software and displayed greater autonomy than their instructors, taking the lead in suggesting how best they participate in classes. Seen through a constructivist lens, placing some control to students' domain is a potential strength of online learning. This is especially true when it leads to increased language output from the students, however that shift can be uncomfortable for the teachers to accept. This shift is something I address in the microblending chapter. The teacher David in Sun Shin's chapter (6) tried several techniques to alter the way students were working and gain the interactivity he had enjoyed in face to face lessons but realised that many of these created more work for little benefit, meanwhile his colleague Kevin felt that he had "more options to make my[his] classes more interesting and relevant for students." which would benefit his teacher after the pandemic. Chris too felt that he was able to increase interaction with the tools he used and was setting more work for his students by the end of the study than his colleagues.

Here both Chris and Kevin seem to have accepted the need to adapt and potentially cede some choice and control to students, working in new ways and doing what I call 'microblending', while David was still showing some of the teacher's fear of loss of control when adopting technology which I have also written about.

4
Where do you see the opportunities and challenges of writing a joint concluding chapter?

JR: It will be really interesting to literally watch while others write their thoughts down, then reflect and redraft our own contributions.

PE: It's an interesting way to bring together, in one place, the joint expertise and concluding reflections of the different authors. The role of the editors will be very important I think in editing the content of this doc, avoiding repetition, and selecting the content they consider most appropriate for publishing as the concluding chapter of the book.

SS: Writing a joint concluding chapter might be challenging to make it flow smoothly and keep all authors' voices alive. However, this project is a great opportunity to reflect on our thoughts and goals for the chapters. Therefore, the joint concluding chapter will provide readers with a clearer picture of this book's purpose and the opportunity to draw on their reflection.

AGR: The whole process of writing a concluding chapter through questions that all authors have to answer is really interesting and challenging, because it forces us to make connections between the different chapters of the book. It also forces us to get out of the narrow view we may have when writing an article or a chapter, and to consider the whole issue of the book. The big challenge will be to transform this multiphonic google doc into a coherent and meaningful text.

JH: I agree with what has been said so far. It's great to have a place where we can have a collective brainstorm of ideas. It will, however, be tricky to tie it all together in one chapter.

HP+KvLS+EV: We find it a great opportunity to collaborate, but we also find it challenging (and time consuming). We also find that doing this from a collaborative document is convenient but feels more like a series of monologues rather than an actual dialogue (for now at least). In this form of collaboration, the final outcome depends heavily on the skilled work of the editors and their interpretation of contributions.

This has allowed us to engage more deeply with the other authors' work and what is going on in the field / the topic of the book, than we would have otherwise.

SH: I think it's nice to come back to it and see the reflections of other contributors. It's good the editors will have an oversight to select and reorder.

DB: The main advantage of such a chapter is that it acts as a digest where the various authors can reflect on the narrative that has emerged from the work co-constructed. While each chapter stands alone, this triangulation of our perspectives of reactions to the pandemic is greater than the sum of its parts. This can serve as a useful guide to the reader and serves to make the volume more accessible. I agree with others that this will need some heavy editing.

5
In helping language teachers to suddenly move their teaching online (Emergency Remote Teaching, ERT), where do you see the benefit of theory? Of evidence based research? Of evaluation or feedback questionnaires? Of literature overviews or reviews? And of toolkits, webinars, or web-based help sites, respectively?

JR: Theory is at the heart of all teaching and learning, not only ERT, whether or not teachers are specifically relating their teaching practice to theory or not. We are hopefully coming to the end of the pandemic and now is a particularly critical time for researchers to remind practitioners about online teaching and learning. There is still a great deal of resistance to online teaching and learning from within the profession and outside too, as if it is somehow a second-best to face-to-face teaching.

PE: Evaluation/Feedback questionnaires can be a very effective way for management teams to understand the issues and challenges teachers have to face in their work. The information received should feed into subsequent course planning and ensure that teachers feel that their hands-on expertise and their opinions are of value.

SS: Teachers want to know whether the way they adapt to online teaching is effective or not, and with detailed feedback, they can also adjust their teaching. Evaluation/Feedback questionnaires would be also helpful for teachers as they seek feedback, especially when they have to adopt a new format in their teaching. Moreover, giving and receiving Evaluation/Feedback can be a part of communication among management, students, and teachers.

AGR: The rapid transition to online education during the pandemic was done in a reactive mode, trying to find quick solutions to the various challenges that suddenly presented themselves to teachers and students.

It is important, however, to move out of this reactive mode, to take stock and make sense of recent experiences of course transition to distance/online modalities. A revisiting of the theoretical framework of online teaching and learning, while also contributing the results of the various surveys conducted during the pandemic to base our thinking on evidence, helps to advance the thinking on effective design and facilitation of teaching and learning in virtual contexts. It also provides a solid foundation for rethinking our pedagogical approaches and practices for virtual education, and for imagining additional learning environments.

JH: I agree that theory, evidence-based research, etc. is central to informing our decisions as teachers and as teacher trainers. And this to a great extent guided us in the design of teacher development initiatives regarding ERT. Due to the urgency of the situation, however, a lot of what was done was based on intuition and common sense, which I feel was completely valid. This pushed us all out of our "comfort zones," forcing us to explore new ways of working with no time to overthink things. Now is the time to reflect in depth on what we did and that's why I believe this book is particularly appropriate and timely.

HP+KvLS+EV: Our approach to developing the toolkit was to turn theory and our research-based knowledge into a tool that was of immediate practical use for language teachers. The theory underpinned the toolkit but was not explicit within it.

In addition, the pandemic was a unique and valuable opportunity for researchers to collect data and observe and analyse teachers' experiences. This will add to theory in the long run.

SH: We quote in our chapter the reflection that pleasure at the success of ERT under the circumstances should not be confused with proper thought-out planning. Toolkits and 'dos' and 'don't' lists were a good off-the-peg, generous, and useful contribution for the immediacy. Reference to theory, even briefly, makes for surer steps with teachers having rationale for day-to-day choices. Limitations such as solid internet access, physical space in the home and availability of devices, of digital and other poverty mean that the utility is not universal.

DB: I think while teachers may seek urgent practical advice, accessible and applicable theory is an essential substrate. The principles teachers were trained under have become quickly obscured by the new priorities of ERT and may find the absence of theory has them teaching in a vacuum. This is part of the loneliness a teacher refers to in chapter 6. Without this underlying roadmap to where they should be trying to reach with remote work, teachers are lost. In my chapter (7) I speak of the need to retain some older established principles of Communicative Language Teaching or Task Based Language Teaching while simultaneously building a technical pedagogic competence. Most teachers seldom come into direct contact with theory, instead finding it applied in the work of syllabus and course book authors or trainers. If these secondary works are written without a common frame of reference such as this volume begins to provide, there can be no cohesive body of informed praxis.

6

In retrospect, what was the most impressive positive response in aiding language teachers during the pandemic in your view? / What helped the most? / What had the greatest impact? What stays with you?

JR: Communities of practice which emerged in social media such as Twitter kept many teachers going; partly with specific advice and recommendations, but also with messages of support for colleagues. A little bit of empathy goes a long way.

SS: The positive thoughts and attitudes of the teachers in my study impressed me. Although they described the beginning of the transition to online teaching as frustrating, they still saw silver linings. While the policies and instructions were confusing or lacking, they tried staying positive, focusing on learning new skills and tools for their students and themselves, and taking this challenging time as an opportunity for self-development and to more deeply connect with students.

PE: I was impressed by the fact that despite having to juggle so many personal and professional challenges during the pandemic, the feedback from surveys and questionnaires indicates that teachers felt, overall, that there was an equilibrium between the positive and negative aspects of their experience during this period.

AGR: First of all, I can only applaud the commitment of the 3500 teachers and teaching assistants at the University of Ottawa who, in this moment of crisis, showed imagination, creativity, courage, and patience (the vast majority had never taught online courses before) to transform their entire teaching online in just one week. What also impressed me a lot was the great collaboration of all the faculties, and the teaching staff, to face and bring solutions to the challenges we were facing every day at the beginning of the pandemic. This collaboration continues: many communities of practice (CoPs) between teachers in the same faculty, or inter-faculty, and even inter-institutional, to share issues, best practices, suggestions, teaching materials etc... has helped to change the perception that the teacher is alone in the classroom. We now see much more co-development of courses, co-teaching, and active CoPs to discuss pedagogy. What teachers also tell us in their responses to the impact surveys we do is that they are much more creative in their pedagogical thinking and more willing to take risks.

JH For me, the most positive outcome has been the huge increase in teachers' digital literacy skills, which occurred in a very short period of time and which was valued favorably by most teachers. In research we have conducted at university language centers in Catalonia, most teachers expressed a desire to continue utilizing aspects of online teaching with their students, rather than to return to pre-pandemic business as usual.

HP+KvLS+EV: What stays with us is the feeling that teachers were keen to come together and support each other. In the toolkit project, the toolkit in itself was clearly invaluable to teachers, but the workshops that were organised to discuss it turned out to be equally, or perhaps more, invaluable. It became obvious that teachers were keen / needed to be part of a community of practice at that time. Incidentally, we organised a 'one year on' workshop (which is not mentioned in our chapter for obvious reasons) which was equally well attended as the initial workshops, demonstrating that such platforms remain useful for teachers for ongoing discussion and sharing of their practice and experience.

We were also extremely impressed with the calm and positive attitude of the teachers who attended our workshops. Their willingness to move their teaching online at short notice and their enthusiasm during the process, even though some of them remained convinced that teaching face-to-face was better than teaching online, were remarkable.

SH: The urge from people who have long been involved in distance learning and language teaching with technology towards initiatives to share bite-size help with the wider language teaching community. The 'Taking your language teaching online' offerings from colleagues at the Open University and ICT-REV team's webcast on the ECML's YouTube channel come to mind for me, because they were on my radar. I am impressed by so many such initiatives.

DB: I agree with Jackie Robbins in that the sharing of best practice powered by the online connectedness we all enjoy through social media gave teachers many of the survival strategies and techniques. Groups such as the four 'lonely' teachers at different Korean universities (Chapter 6) can benefit hugely from sharing their collective experiences as a Personal Learning Network (PLN). I am seeing more and more of this happening, with some teachers starting questions in social media posts as 'Dear PLN...'.

I do feel we owe a debt to the response of the private sector with *Zoom* and *Google Classroom* tools, for example offering cheap or free access to high quality Computer Mediated Communication (CMC) tools that were used internationally. This put industry standard tools in the hands of teachers. This kind of open access led to de-facto standards with classroom formats. Thousands of teachers and trainers worldwide became familiar with features such as breakout rooms and spotlighting, with these becoming normalised as common practice.

What did we take away (editors' reflections)?

Although the idea for a collaborative final chapter was incepted during the planning of this book, the chapter itself emerged iteratively and hence is not based on preconceived editor notions. We as editors were prepared to take the risk of not knowing what we would get from this chapter, because we had hoped that the outcome would exceed our expectations - and it did! Giving authors the opportunity to reflect upon their own writing as well as on the work of other contributors provides a different and intensive way for authors to identify with a book and to make it their own. The asynchronous writing process over a designated period of time allows for a more nuanced reflection of one's own position, although the degree to which this has happened may differ for different authors, depending on the extent to which the contributions of the other authors are visible - or not - at the time of writing. Last but not least, writing a collaborative final chapter is about equality and voices; instead of the editorial voice, the voices of all authors conclude this book. Based on this positive experience, the editors have decided to implement a collective book chapter in all future publications of the book series *Developing Online Language Pedagogies*.

Finally, this book is our contribution to making the move to online language teaching sustainable and lasting. The immense effort of teachers, teacher trainers, technology experts and institutions in switching to "Emergency Remote Teaching" at the drop of a hat should not go to waste. We have gathered the voices of experts who did their bit in helping during the crisis and now have the time to reflect on what of those changes, enforced and created, will be lasting and worth sustaining. The crisis has made it widely known that online language teaching is possible, that it can be effective and successful and even enjoyable. The future will definitely be more of a blend of teaching in physically shared spaces and physically distributed (often online) spaces. To prepare language teachers for this future, we wish to highlight the need for solid training, the development of specific online teaching skills for language teachers and the requirement for *ad hoc*, on demand staff development. The shared experience of creating this volume in times of crisis while gathering impressive evidence of teacher creativity will become a lasting memory and a beacon to guide us in "Developing" future "Online Language Pedagogies."

Index

affordance, 12, 66, 71–74, 77
application/app, 18, 50, 54, 58, 78, 89, 105, 106
assessment, xii, xiii, 10, 16, 19, 20, 68, 72, 101, 110,
autonomy, xiii, 31, 32, 36, 110, 1221

British Council, 16, 17, 19, 24,
burnout, 82, 83

Chegg Prep, 109
Community of Inquiry (CoI), 13
community, xii, xiv, 13, 14, 19, 20, 33, 34, 40, 48, 52, 54, 55, 61, 65–67, 78, 114, 119, 126
    learning, 13, 33, 40
    online, 1, 20, 68, 75,
    sense of, 34, 62, 72, 73, 75, 121
    teaching, 94, 121, 126
competence, 14, 75, 125
    communicative, 70, 72–76, 78
    ICT, 70, 72, 77
    intercultural, 11
    teaching, 9
    technical, 70, 72, 77
computer-assisted language learning (CALL), 65, 76
computer-mediated communication (CMC), 127
confidence, 1, 9, 14, 16, 36, 47, 55, 56–61, 72, 73, 89, 104, 120, 121
coping strategies, xi, xii, 1, 4, 46, 47, 82–86, 88, 91–93
Covid-19, 1, 2, 8, 11, 13, 14, 16, 18–21, 45, 46, 48, 58, 64, 67–69, 74–78, 82–85, 98, 99, 102, 109 113
    pre-Covid-19, 28,
    post-Covid-19, 90

dialogue, xii, xiii, 7, 31–33, 36, 38–41, 51, 114, 123
Digital Learning Directors, 14
digital literacy, 9–11, 18, 126
digital tool, 18, 83, 90, 99
distance
    learning, xii, 8, 9, 12, 15, 17, 19, 31, 32, 36, 37, 39, 48, 85, 117, 126
    pedagogical, 31, 35
    psychological, 31, 34
DOTS, 38, 47
Dropbox, 54, 109

English for Academic Purposes (EAP), 108
Engage, Study, Active (ESA), 107, 109
English for Special Purposes (ESP), 87, 108
English as a Foreign Language (EFL), 10, 105
e-learning, 10, 12, 30–33, 40, 41
European Centre for Modern Languages (ECML/CELV), 15, 16, 18, 21, 25, 28, 38, 47, 49, 50, 53, 59, 117, 120, 126
Emergency remote teaching (ERT), x–xiii, 13, 120, 123–125
engagement
    emotional, 48, 60, 61
    student, 10, 19, 20, 29, 30, 35
experience, 1, 5, 8–10, 12–19, 20, 21, 34, 38, 39, 45–48, 51–55, 61, 62, 64, 65, 68–72, 74–78, 83, 85, 87–91, 99–101, 109, 113, 116, 117, 119, 120, 124–127
    learning, 15, 29, 30, 33, 34, 41, 116
    online, 34
    teaching, 35, 36, 85

Index

Facebook, 19, 721
face-to-face/f2f, x, 2, 10, 14, 19, 28, 29, 31, 33, 37, 47–52, 54, 55, 59, 61, 66, 67, 69, 74–76, 84, 86, 98, 99, 102, 105, 109, 118, 119, 123
feedback, xiv, xv, 7, 11, 12, 14, 20, 21, 29, 34, 36, 60, 93, 123–125

Google Docs, xv, 35, 54, 105, 109, 114, 115, 123
Google Meet, 49
Google Slides, 102

hybrid, 28, 29, 41, 118

ICT-REV, x, 18, 38, 47–50, 52–55, 57, 59, 61, 116, 117, 120, 1276
Information and Communication Technology (ICT), x, 11, 18, 21, 45, 47, 48, 50–53, 57, 59, 61, 70, 72, 78, 98
interaction, xiv, xv, 11, 13, 18, 20, 29, 33–37, 41, 46, 50, 61, 65, 66, 69, 72, 73, 88, 89, 93, 101, 105, 122

Jitsi, 49

Kahoot, 10, 54, 56, 58, 106
Keynote, 102

learner-centred, 45, 65, 121
learning management system, 10, 18, 30, 66, 68
locus of control, 93
low-tech, 105

Mentimeter, 51, 54–56, 60
microblending, 4, 98, 99, 100, 102, 103, 106, 107, 109, 110, 120–122
Microsoft Teams, 19, 39, 49
MOOCs, 14, 18, 20
Moodle, 54
motivation, xii, 5, 16, 18, 20, 29, 30, 34 –37, 41, 46, 67, 68, 113

needs
  learners', 66, 68, 98
  teachers', 3, 17, 60, 61
  students', *see* needs, learners

Optical Character Recognition (OCR), 102
online
  teaching, xi, xii, xiv, 1, 2, 4–6, 9, 11–13, 15, 17, 20, 21, 28, 29, 34-37, 39, 40, 46, 47, 52, 64–69, 74–79, 82–85, 87, 89, 91–93, 99–101, 109, 110, 116–121, 124, 126–127
  learning, x, xiii, 9–12, 14–16, 30, 31, 33–35, 40, 41, 47, 65, 68, 99, 116, 122
  education, x, xii, 12, 14, 29, 30–32, 58, 120, 121
  environment, 5, 30-32, 39–41, 66
  material, 65 102, 110
  platform, xiii, 67, 99, 103, 108
open educational resources (OERs), 21
open educational practice (OEP), 21

Padlet, 35, 53, 55, 60, 71
PowerPoint, 102, 107
presence, xiii, 3, 28, 29, 30, 32-34, 36-41, 119, 120
  psychological, 35
  social, 13, 20, 33
  socio-affective, xiii, 33, 40
  teaching, 66, 68
professional development, xi, xii, 3, 8, 9, 11, 15, 16, 19, 21, 29, 38, 41, 42, 45, 47, 48, 62, 78, 100, 113, 116–118
professional isolation, 19
proximity, 3, 29–33, 36–41, 119–121

Quizlet, 56, 106, 109

remote learning, 8, 14, 84, 85

self-development, 89, 91, 125
self-directed learning, 18
self-efficacy, 89
skills pyramid, 3, 65, 67, 69, 70, 74, 76, 77–79

Skype, 12, 49, 54
socio-cultural theories, 2, 65
stressor, xii, 2, 4, 82, 83, 85, 86, 90–93
support
  administrative, xiv, 86–88
  peer, 16
  psychosocial, 18
  social, xii, 83
  synchronous, 19
  technical, xv, 50, 61, 84, 92

task-based, 65, 105, 107, 109
teacher agency, 99, 110
teacher training, x, xi, xv, 3, 5, 8, 11, 14, 17, 19, 21, 38, 40, 65, 78, 100, 106, 121
teacher wellbeing, xi, 3, 16, 82, 83, 93, 113
Toolkit, 3, 6, 20, 21, 64, 65, 67–69, 75, 76, 78–80, 117, 119, 121, 123, 124, 126
Technology Pedagogic Content Knowledge (TPCK), 100

UNESCO, 12, 17, 26, 64

virtual learning, 13, 14
virtual learning environments (VLEs), 8
videoconferencing, 39, 50, 54, 102
video-streaming, xi, 3, 10

webinar, 16, 18–21, 45, 48, 50–61, 118 –121, 123
WhatsApp, 10, 11, 721

YouTube, 10, 35, 45, 50, 54, 55, 60, 61, 117, 126

Zoom, 10, 11, 19, 49, 50, 54, 56, 102, 119, 127

www.ingramcontent.com/pod-product-compliance
Lightning Source LLC
Chambersburg PA
CBHW051543230426
43669CB00015B/2701